*Shining the Light on Coercive Control: See It. Survive
It. Change It.*
www.coercivecontrolspotlight.com

**First published in 2025 by**
Rebecca Sarah-Jane Stuttard
Edited by Melissa Maher
Contribution by Cara Pullen

**ISBN (Paperback):** 9781764327602
**ISBN (eBook):** 9781764327619
**Legal deposit: National eDeposit (NED), 2025.**
Available via the National Library of Australia and participating
State and Territory Librarie

**Content and Legal Disclaimer**
This book, which is provided for educational and awareness purposes
only, is based on the author's lived experience and professional
perspective.
It does not constitute legal, medical, or therapeutic advice, and the
author and publisher accept no liability for reliance on its content.
Support is available at 1800RESPECT (1800 737 732)

1

## BISAC Subject Headings:

FAM001030 – FAMILY & RELATIONSHIPS / Abuse / Domestic Partner Abuse
FAM000000 – FAMILY & RELATIONSHIPS / General
FAM034000 – FAMILY & RELATIONSHIPS / Parenting / General
FAM013000 – FAMILY & RELATIONSHIPS / Conflict Resolution
PSY022040 – PSYCHOLOGY / Trauma & Post-Traumatic Stress Disorder
PSY020000 – PSYCHOLOGY / Mental Health
PSY010000 – PSYCHOLOGY / Interpersonal Relations
SEL031000 – SELF-HELP / Personal Growth / General
SEL011000 – SELF-HELP / Abuse / General
SOC028000 – SOCIAL SCIENCE / Women's Studies
SOC004000 – SOCIAL SCIENCE / Violence in Society
LAW038000 – LAW / Family Law / General

## Preface & Introduction

Coercive control is a pattern of behaviour used to dominate, isolate, and entrap another person. Often invisible to outsiders, it strips victims of freedom, safety, and identity. For too long, people have failed to recognise it as a serious violation of human rights, dismissing it as a private matter instead.

## The Lens I Write Through

I write as a survivor, a professional, a mother, and a law student determined to make the system safer. Coercive control has profoundly shaped my life—not only through the abuse itself but also through the repeated failures of the very systems I once trusted to protect me.

That suffering, however, also forged my passion. Today, I am fiercely committed to educating and advocating for better recognition and response to coercive control. Survivors often describe coercive control, rather than physical assaults, as the most devastating part of domestic violence. The ongoing manipulation, indoctrination, and psychological captivity erode selfhood and keep victims trapped.

Many do not even recognise what they are experiencing until they are outside the situation, when patterns become clearer in hindsight. Therefore, it is vital for professionals—police, lawyers, social workers, educators, and health practitioners—to be equipped with adequate training to recognise coercive control. Early recognition could save and change lives.

I hope that by sharing both my lived experience and professional insights, this book will shed light on coercive control, equipping readers to recognise it when they see it, and inspiring the development of systems that truly protect and empower those at risk.

## My First Book: A Silenced Voice

This work builds on my first published book, which I wrote after a near-death experience compelled me to give voice to the injustices I had witnessed. Within months, I had written and published it—despite advice that such a rapid process was not the norm. Looking back, I realise how headstrong I was, writing without fully considering the long-term implications, particularly for my children, despite using de-identification.

I was told to cease the sale of the book soon after its release, or face legal action if I did not comply, as per family law. I felt as though someone had ripped away the voice I had rediscovered after a lifetime of silence. That experience forced me to confront the absence of an express right to free speech in our federal Constitution. Could the limited protections of religious freedom have shielded my freedom of expression? I believed God had called me to write the book, yet the legal system silenced me.

## Legal Reform: Where We Stand

In recent years, states in Australia have introduced specific offences related to coercive control.

New South Wales passed coercive control legislation in 2022, starting operation in July 2024. However, the law initially limits itself to current or former intimate partner relationships. This leaves a critical gap: children and extended family members who may also be victims of controlling behaviour fall outside statutory protection.

Queensland followed with the Criminal Law (Coercive Control and Affirmative Consent) and Other Legislation Amendment Act 2024), criminalising coercive control within domestic/family relationships and establishing definitions and sentencing frameworks. However, it also focuses primarily on an intimate partner framework.

Western Australia has announced a phased approach, progressing reforms and system changes without yet enacting a merged offence.

This uneven rollout across states and territories means that protecting victims and subsequent offences available to the police still depend on residential location.

**Terminology and Contested Views**

Several terms and debates remain highly contested across multiple areas of research and practice in family law, child protection, and domestic and family violence. These debates matter because the language we use shapes how professionals, courts, and services respond to families.

**Parental Alienation:** The term 'parental alienation' remains controversial, dividing professionals because of its origins and application; an issue I remain impartial towards. Personally, I believe they have similarities: family and domestic violence, coercive control, emotional, psychological, and child abuse are all patterns of power imbalance and manipulation. They are serious crimes, regardless of the language framework.

**Gendered Violence** People also ask if family and domestic violence is inherently gendered. Research often highlights male-perpetrated violence against women; however, I do not adopt a gender-exclusive perspective. From my professional experience as a first-response domestic violence counsellor, I understand that all people, regardless of sex at birth, gender identity, or age, can be victims. Coercive controlling dynamics can occur in all relationships.

This inclusive, experienced approach informs how I discuss and analyse coercive control throughout this book.

Throughout, you will see recurring sections designed to weave together lived experience, professional insight, and research:

**My journey**: reflections drawn from my own lived experience.

**From the Therapy Room**: stories, tools, and insights from my professional work.

**Self-Reflection**: guided prompts and gentle exercises for your own growth.

**Research Insights**: summaries of key findings that illuminate patterns of coercive control.

You are welcome to proceed through these at your own pace, as they best serve you. For example, you may choose to skip the research summaries if they feel heavy or return to the self-reflection exercises later when you feel ready.

Language in family and domestic violence is powerful and deeply personal. Some people identify strongly with the word victim, others with survivor, while many feel neither captures their total experience. In this book, I use the terms' victim-survivor' and 'victim' to acknowledge both the harm experienced and resilience.

For clarity and consistency, I use gender-neutral pronouns (they/them) and parent.

I refer to post-separation abuse, recognising how abuse often escalates when parents share children.

I use the terms perpetrator and abuser in line with legal terminology to emphasise the asymmetry of power and responsibility.

These choices reflect both professional practice and the reality that the words we use matter; they shape not only understanding but also how people feel seen, validated, and protected.

## Gentle Note

This book is here to share my experiences, support, and encourage reflection. It is not a substitute for therapy, crisis support, legal advice, or medical care.

The personal reflections come from my life and work. I hope that through my sharing, you will learn something worthwhile or not feel alone. My book may not be suitable for every situation or individual. If you feel unsafe, overwhelmed, or triggered, it is okay to stop reading and take care of yourself. You might:

Reach out to a trusted friend or support person.

Contact a GP, psychologist, or counsellor.

Call a domestic violence helpline or crisis line in your area.

The book lists key support services towards the end. Please remember to use what feels helpful, leave what does not, and always prioritise your physical and mental safety and wellbeing.

# Acknowledgements

To the tribe of people who walk beside me, often lending me your strength when I felt I had none, I am forever grateful and blessed — my family, my people, my anchors.

Life's most challenging moments have shaped me in ways I never expected. Though painful, they carved out spaces where resilience, compassion, and purpose could grow. I hold close the wisdom that our falls do not define us, but by how we rise, rebuild, and choose to live in truth.

I am grateful to serve in purpose through God, whose presence continues to guide my steps and steady my heart. To my children, the reason I found my strength, and the home of my love. My life transformed the day I became a mother. You will be in my heart forever. A mother's love knows no limits, and mine for you will never fade.

# Part One
# Making the Invisible Visible

## Understanding Your Window of Tolerance

Before we explore the Window of Tolerance, please pause for a moment and gently turn your attention inward. This first chapter serves as an invitation to cultivate an awareness of your body and feelings, enabling you to notice what arises within you as you read and reflect. The Window of Tolerance is not only a way to understand trauma response but also a tool you can apply to everyday life. You can also use it to recognise your feelings of steadiness, of being stretched, and of needing care.

### Where This Concept Comes From

Dr Dan Siegel, a clinical professor of psychiatry and a pioneer in interpersonal neurobiology, introduced the term Window of Tolerance. Siegel used this phrase to describe the zone in which we manage stress and remain engaged with life.

When we are within this window, our brains can work at their best. We can think clearly, manage our emotions, solve problems, and make moral decisions. We can also feel more connected to ourselves and others.

However, when we step outside this window, our bodies switch into a state of survival mode. This may manifest as hyperarousal, also known as the fight-or-flight response. This can present as anxiety, panic, anger, or being on high alert. It can also present as hypoarousal: a kind of shutdown, where one may feel numb, disconnected, or collapsed. In both states, it is much harder to think clearly or manage emotions. This can explain why even minor stressors or reminders of trauma may feel so overwhelming.

Today, trauma therapists widely use this framework because it explains why survivors may struggle with regulation, even in moments that seem safe to others. It reminds us that these reactions are not weaknesses; they are natural survival responses of the body and brain to stress and trauma.

### Visualising Your Window:

Metaphors and images can make the Window of Tolerance easier to grasp. In this book, I use the ocean to visualise the concept. Our emotions are like waves in that they rise and fall, sometimes calm and sometimes stormy, sometimes in between. No state is permanent, and just as waves always return to the middle waters, we too can find our way back to balance.

### The Ocean Metaphor

Imagine your nervous system as an ocean with three levels:

**Surface Waters:** Hyperarousal: Rough waves. This is fight-or-flight mode. You may feel anxious, panicky, angry, jittery, have racing thoughts, or have a pounding heart. Your body signals, Danger! Act now! **Middle Waters**: Window of Tolerance: Calm enough to float. You can breathe, see clearly, and respond thoughtfully. However, the middle waters may not always be perfectly calm. You can still feel activated or dysregulated in this space- but always have access to choices.

**Deep Waters:** Hypoarousal: Heavy, still, dark waters. This is the freeze or shutdown state. You may feel numb, foggy, dissociated, or exhausted.

Not everyone connects with the same imagery as their own window of tolerance, and that is okay. The important thing is to choose an image that helps you notice where you are and what you need to return to balance. Many of the children I have worked with seem to resonate with the concept of the volcano. Other metaphors I have come across are.

**Weather System**

Clear sunny day = regulated

Thunderstorm = fight/flight

Fog or snow = freeze

**Music / Rhythm**

Steady beat = regulated

Racing beat or loud distortion = fight/flight

Muted or silent = freeze

**Lantern / Light**

Steady glow = regulated

Flickering flame = fight/flight

Almost out = freeze

**Battery / Energy**

Balanced charge = regulated
Overheating = fight/flight
Shut down = freeze

**Gentle Note:** If you rarely experience what I refer to as calm middle waters, you are in good company. It simply means your nervous system has been working very hard to keep you safe. With care, practice, and support, your window can expand again.

## Emotional Flashbacks

Sometimes, leaving your window of tolerance is not about what is happening right now, but your past being activated. You can refer to these moments as emotional flashbacks. Your nervous system responds as if it is back in the original danger, flooding you with intense feelings from that earlier time. When you notice this happening, gently acknowledging it can help you reconnect with the present and guide yourself back into your window of tolerance. When someone pushes you outside your window, it is not just in your head. Regulation is about sending your body the message: you are safe enough to come back.

## The Role of the Vagus Nerve

The vagus nerve is the longest cranial nerve in the body, stretching from the brainstem through the neck, chest, and into the abdomen. It connects with nearly every major organ, including the heart, lungs, and digestive system, serving as a vital information highway between the body and brain.

This nerve is a cornerstone of the parasympathetic nervous system, often referred to as the "rest-and-digest" branch. Its job is to help the body recover after stress. When activated, the vagus nerve sends a powerful message of safety to the brain. In response, your heart rate slows, your breath deepens, digestion restarts, and the body shifts out of survival mode into a state of calm.

### Why This Matters for Trauma Survivors:

When you have experienced chronic stress or been a victim or survivor of coercive control, your nervous system can get stuck in fight, flight, or freeze. Activating the vagus nerve is one way to tell the body, It is okay to come back to safety now. With practice, these small signals of safety strengthen your resilience and gradually make it easier to remain within your window of tolerance.

### Ways to Stimulate the Vagus Nerve

You do not need special equipment; simply employing gentle, everyday activities can send signals of safety to your body and brain.

### Breathwork

Slow, steady breathing, long exhalations, activates the vagus nerve. Techniques such as box breathing (inhale for 4 seconds, hold for 4 seconds, exhale for 4 seconds, hold for 4 seconds) or 4-7-8 breathing can be especially calming.

### Sound & Vibration

Humming, chanting, or singing can create vibrations in the throat that stimulate the vagus nerve. Even gentle humming can help shift your body toward a state of calm.

**Gentle Pressure**
Placing a hand over your heart, lightly massaging your neck, or using a weighted blanket can stimulate vagal pathways and increase a sense of safety.

**Cold Exposure**
Splashing cool water on your face, holding an ice cube, or applying a cool compress can trigger the dive reflex, which slows the heart rate and calms the nervous system.

**Social Connection**
Maintaining safe eye contact, engaging in soft conversation, or co-regulating with a trusted person activates the vagus nerve, reinforcing feelings of safety and connection.

**Building Vagal Tone**
Like exercise strengthens muscles, regular vagus nerve stimulation strengthens your nervous system's ability to return to calm after stress. This does not mean you will never feel triggered. It just means that over time, your body learns how to settle more quickly and reliably.

The practices below originated in trauma therapy, neuroscience, and somatic psychology. They help your nervous system return to a state of safety and re-enter your window of tolerance. Move slowly, try them one at a time, and notice which practices feel supportive. If something feels too much, pause and choose a gentler option.

## Grounding Through the Senses

When you feel overwhelmed, focusing on your immediate surroundings can help pull you back into the present moment.

5-4-3-2-1 Technique:

Name

5 things you can see

4 things you can touch

3 things you can hear

2 things you can smell

1 thing you can taste

These simple exercises interrupt spirals of fear and reestablish a sense of the present moment.

## Gentle Movement & Shaking

Animals often shake after escaping danger to discharge adrenaline and regain their equilibrium. Humans can also benefit from this.

Try: Gently shake out your arms and legs.

Take a mindful walk, focusing on each step as you move.

Stretch your arms overhead, or fold forward and let your body flop.

## Safe Touch & Pressure

Grounding, touch, and pressure signal safety to your body and release oxytocin, the hormone of connection.

Try:

Wrapping yourself in a weighted blanket.

Place one hand on your chest and one on your belly, breathing slowly.

## Bilateral Stimulation

Therapists also use this technique in therapies like Eye Movement Desensitisation and Reprocessing (EMDR), which helps people process distressing memories and calm the nervous system.

Try:

Cross your arms over your chest and gently tap left, right, left, right?

Walk slowly while paying attention to the rhythm of alternating steps.

Listen to bilateral music with headphones (alternating tones).

## Co-Regulation (If Safe)

Sometimes, our nervous system needs another to feel safe.

Try:

Call a trusted friend who can stay calm with you.

Sit with a safe person or pet.

If appropriate, ask for a steady, grounding hug

## Practising Self-Compassion

Research shows self-compassion lowers stress hormones and supports regulation. Speaking kindly to yourself can rewire old patterns of self-criticism.

Try saying:

I am safe enough right now.

My body is reacting, and that is okay.

I can take my time before I respond.

If this feels hard, imagine how you would comfort a close friend, then offer those exact words to yourself.

## Slow, Rhythmic Breathing

Breathing is one of the fastest ways to influence your nervous system. Long exhalations activate the parasympathetic system, signalling to your body that it is safe.

Try this:

Inhale through your nose for a count of four.

Hold gently for one.

Exhale through your mouth for a count of six.

## Self-Reflection: Mapping Your Window

Take a moment to pause and gently check in with yourself. You may prefer to write your answers in a journal or sketch them out as a visual representation of your nervous system.

Body Clues: Where do you usually feel it when you leave your Window of Tolerance? (Chest, stomach, shoulders, jaw, head?)

Direction: Do you go up (fight/flight, racing thoughts, restlessness, anger) or down (freeze, shut down, numbness, fatigue)?

Regulation Helpers: What has helped you come back into your window before? (Deep breathing, talking to a friend, writing things down, moving your body?)

As you practice these tools, be aware of the minor changes over time that may show you can recover more quickly after being triggered. You may even feel calmer in situations that used to overwhelm you. These shifts are signs that your window of tolerance is widening. Celebrate these moments. Each one means your nervous system is learning that safety is possible again.

## My journey

I have two distinct responses when I slip outside my window of tolerance — and yes; it is entirely possible to move between them, depending on what is happening around me. The body remembers what safety feels like, but it also remembers what threat feels like, and sometimes, it reacts before the mind has time to catch up.

When I am in hyperarousal, it is as if I am treading water at the surface of a restless sea. Adrenaline floods my system; my chest tightens, and my shoulders lift toward my ears as though bracing for impact. My words rush out faster than I can catch them — a blur of energy and urgency — while my thoughts bounce like pinballs, one colliding into another.

In those moments, my nervous system is searching for release. Movement becomes medicine. I will slip on my headphones and head into the garden, pulling weeds with Olympic determination, or I will rearrange furniture until the space feels new again — a surprisingly common ADHD coping strategy, I have since learned. Physical action helps my body discharge the excess energy, making room for steadiness to return.

**Freeze** feels like sinking beneath the surface. Everything slows—my thoughts, my voice, and even my awareness blur. In the past, I would drift so far into stillness that I wanted to watch my life from somewhere outside of myself. It happens less often now, but when it does, I meet it with gentleness.

I ground myself in small, sensory ways:

- Taking slow, deliberate breaths
- Stroking the soft fur of my companions, Chanel and Indy
- Holding a cool drink or splashing water on my face
- Humming quietly or pressing my palms together until I feel present again

These simple rituals remind my body that it is safe now — that it no longer needs to fight or flee or disappear. Healing, for me, has been learning that both states — the racing and the stillness — are messages from the nervous system asking for care, not punishment.

### The Power of Simply Noticing

Sometimes the most I can do is say to myself, I am out of my window right now. Honestly, that is powerful. The moment I notice it; I am no longer completely lost; I am observing it. Awareness, even in small doses, is one of the gentlest forms of regulation there is.

## From the Therapy Room

From a professional perspective, having tangible tools can make an enormous difference. Sometimes words alone are not enough to bring someone back into their body.

I keep what I call my balance bag. Inside are simple, everyday items that help bring the body back to the present:

Fidgets: a collection of stress balls, putty, squishy toys, clickers, and tangles, each with a different texture or resistance. Other clients prefer distinct sensations, so variety means there is usually something that feels right.

Grounding objects include smooth stones, feathers, or textured fabric swatches that individuals can hold, stroke, or trace with their fingers.

Creative Supplies: Textas, markers, and paper so people can draw, doodle, or scribble big, angry lines to express what words cannot capture.

Aroma and Sensory Items: Calming scents (such as lavender sachets) or stimulating ones (like peppermint) can help people either slow down from hyperarousal or wake up from a state of freeze.

When we are dysregulated, it can feel impossible to think our way back into calm: the body usually needs to be engaged first. A fidget in the hand, a marker moving across paper, or the simple act of squeezing putty can help discharge energy or re-anchor awareness in the present moment.

I often encourage my clients to build their own personal regulation kits at home. This could be a small basket, bag, or box filled with items that help them feel safe and grounded. What works one day may not work the next. Having a range of tools means you can choose something that matches your state in the moment: something to calm down, something to wake up, or something to keep you company until the storm passes.

Your kit does not need to be fancy or expensive. It only needs to hold what feels grounding to you. Over time, experimenting with these tools can become an integral part of your healing journey, a creative process of discovering what your nervous system responds to.

**A Gentle note**

Your nervous system may require additional support. Working with a trauma-informed therapist can help you gently widen your window and feel safer in your body.

You do not have to use all these tools at once. Choose one or two that feel doable in the moment. The goal is not to be perfectly calm, but to move closer to the middle calm water zone. Here, your body can settle, and your mind can think clearly enough to respond safely.

# Understanding Coercive Control

The Legal Dictionary of Australian Law defines coercive control as: "a pattern of behaviours in an intimate or family relationship that should dominate, isolate, or control another person, which may include physical, psychological, financial, or sexual abuse, and which may occur with or without physical violence."

Coercive control is not about a single argument or a one-off act of violence. It is a deliberate pattern of behaviour designed to dominate, isolate, and entrap another person. Over time, this pattern erodes the victim's autonomy, confidence, and sense of safety.

While coercive control may include physical violence, it often operates through non-physical tactics such as threats, intimidation, surveillance, financial restrictions, and psychological manipulation. These tactics are ongoing and systematic, and they may make the victim feel monitored or limited in every part of their life.

Professor Evan Stark brought into focus the concept, whose landmark book Coercive Control: How Men Entrap Women in Personal Life (2007) shifted how we understand abuse. Stark argued that domestic abuse is not best explained as isolated incidents, but as an entire system of domination that shapes the victim's everyday reality.

One of the key differences between coercive control and other forms of abuse is that it builds up. An assault or angry outburst may be sudden, but coercive control is ongoing, insidious, deliberate, and relentless. It seeps into daily life, limiting choices, straining relationships, and controlling access to resources. This is how it can trap victims, even when there are no visible signs of violence.

## The 9 Masks of Coercive Control

Coercive control rarely shows up as overt domination at the beginning of a relationship. Instead, it develops through behaviours that, on the surface, may appear caring and protective. Survivors often describe the sense of living with multiple versions of the same person, each with distinct faces that can change depending on the current situation.

To make sense of this, I describe these patterns as the nine masks of coercive control. Each mask represents a tactic that can appear on its own or, more often, layered with others. Together, they erode autonomy, isolate, and create dependence. By naming these masks, we can see coercive control not as random arguments or bad moods, but as a deliberate system of domination.

### 1. The Charmer

Love-bombing, fast-tracking intimacy, grand gestures.

Presents as attentive, generous, too good to be true.

Impact: creates rapid trust and emotional investment.

### 2. The Isolator

Cuts the victim off from friends, family, and support, sometimes subtly, sometimes overtly.

Frames isolation as love; I want you all to myself, or as conflict; your friends are jealous of how much I love you and our connection.

Impact: reduces outside perspectives and increases dependency.

### 3. The Critic

Uses put-downs, sarcasm, or jokes to undermine confidence.

Targets appearance, intelligence, parenting, or choices.

Impact: erodes self-esteem, causing the victim to doubt their own worth.

### 4. The Gaslighter

Denies facts, twists reality, and makes the victim question their memory or sanity

Repeats false claims until they feel true.

Impact: destabilises and makes the victim rely on the perpetrator's version of reality.

### 5. The Controller

Micro-manages daily life, money, phone use, clothing, routines, even sleep or eating.

Rules may change without notice, keeping the victim in hypervigilance.

Impact: creates dependence.

## 6. The Watcher

Monitors messages, tracks movements, and demands proof of whereabouts.

Uses jealousy and suspicion as justification.

Impact: instils fear of being constantly under surveillance.

## 7. The Manipulator

Uses guilt, pity, I do not have anyone else, threats of self-harm, or sudden anger to win compliance.

Shifts between victimhood and aggression.

Impact: keeps the victim responsible for their emotions and behaviour, never takes accountability.

## 8. The Intimidator

Relies on anger, shouting, threats, destruction of property, or actual violence.

May follow up with conditional kindness.

Impact: The intimidator mask reinforces fear and signals the cost of resistance, keeping the

The victim remains trapped in a cycle of anxiety and false hope.

## 9. The Jailer

The culmination of multiple tactics leaves the victim feeling trapped.

Leaving seems impossible because of finances, children, threats, shame, or loss of identity, often because of dependence.

Impact: creates long-term entrapment and maintains power at all costs.

## The Invisible Chains of Coercive Control

Evan Stark employs the imagery of invisible chains to illustrate that coercive control extends beyond physical barriers, encompassing emotional and psychological chains that restrict freedom, autonomy, and selfhood.

These chains tighten through layers of internal struggle.

Fear: the constant threat, often unspoken, of harm, retaliation, or escalation

Guilt & Shame: being manipulated into feeling responsible for the abuse or believing that you deserve it

Confusion/doubt: gaslighting that undermines your memory, perception, or sense of reality

Hope: intermittent kindness or promises that things will change, offering a mirage of safety

Each link is invisible, yet as real as iron in its constraining and trapping power.

## What Drives Coercive Control?

Coercive control is not accidental; it is intentional. At its core, power, entitlement, and the belief that one person has a right to dominate another.

While factors such as cultural norms, trauma histories, or brain wiring may influence behaviour, they do not excuse it. Coercive control is never merely about anger, alcohol, or stress. These may be tools or excuses, but the root is a belief in power and dominance.

Understanding this helps us move beyond myths such as 'it was just stress' and see coercive control for what it is: a calculated system of domination, not random acts of cruelty.

## History and Recognition in Law and Policy

Coercive control has gained recognition as the organising feature of family and domestic violence. The Power and Control Wheel, developed by the Duluth Project in the 1980s, remains one of the most influential models of this, mapping tactics such as intimidation, isolation, economic abuse, and threats.

Internationally, the UK criminalised coercive or controlling behaviour in 2015 under the Serious Crime Act, reframing abuse as a pattern rather than a single incident. Canada, the US, and parts of Europe now reference coercive control in family law and risk assessments.

Australia has been slower. Tasmania was the first Australian state or territory to legislate against non-physical abuse through the Family Violence Act 2004. Still, it took almost three years before they meaningfully applied the provisions. This was primarily because of a limited understanding of how coercive control operates in practice.

New South Wales followed with the Crimes Legislation Amendment (Coercive Control) Act 2022, which began in 2024 but applies only to current or former intimate partners, excluding children, siblings, carers, and others in family-like relationships.

Queensland's reforms in 2024 created a specific offence for coercive control in domestic and family relationships. The tireless advocacy of victims' families and campaigners has shaped this move following the horrific murder of Hannah Clarke and her three children in 2020. The Hannah Clarke reforms have become a touchstone for recognising coercive control as a precursor to lethal violence.

Western Australia is trialling training and pilot measures before legislating, signalling a phased approach.

National advocates have also fuelled the push for reform, such as Rosie Batty, whose public leadership following the murder of her son Luke in 2014 reframed family violence as a national crisis. Her advocacy has kept coercive control and systemic reform on the public agenda. This will ensure that law and policy move beyond narrow definitions of violence, addressing patterns that entrap and endanger families.

## Difference Between Coercive Control and Other Forms of Abuse

Coercive control is distinct from other abuse types because it is persistent and relational. Its goal is not just to hurt, but to structure a victim's world around the perpetrator's power.

You can summarise the difference:

**Persistence:** continuous pattern, not a one-off incident.

**Relational Target**: Seeks to reorganise the victim's autonomy and choices.

**Psychological Impact**: Creates fear, guilt, and dependency.

**System manipulation**: exploits courts, agencies, and laws to maintain dominance.

**Invisibility** explains why police, courts, and even friends/family often miss it.

**Entrapment reinforces** Stark's concept of invisible chains and shows that the goal is not harm for its own sake, but long-term domination.

### Psychological Impact on Survivors

Coercive control can function as captivity: not with bars or chains, but invisible restrictions shaping a survivor's every thought, choice, and action. The psychological toll can mirror what prisoners of war or hostages endure:

**Hypervigilance**: constantly scanning the environment, braced for the next shift in mood or danger

**Dissociation:** feeling numb, detached, or watching oneself from the outside to survive

**Walking on eggshells**: the constant, exhausting effort to avoid triggering anger or punishment

Over time, these patterns not only shape how survivors behave but also reshape their self-perception and worldview. This can create a climate of fear and self-doubt that lingers long after the relationship ends. Many develop post-traumatic stress responses (PTSD), depression, or anxiety, often alongside feelings of shame and worthlessness.

Some survivors cope by minimising awareness of the abuse, a response described in betrayal trauma research as adaptive unawareness. Part of the mind dulls the impact just enough for day-to-day survival. This survival response can make recognising coercive control exceedingly difficult until the survivor is physically or emotionally removed from the situation.

## Health Consequences

The constant stress of living under coercive control takes a serious toll on the body. When the nervous system must remain in survival mode, the stress response remains activated. This chronic activation disrupts core body systems, such as.Sleep: insomnia, restless nights, or waking frequently from hyper-alertness

Digestion can cause gut pain, nausea, or poor nutrient absorption because blood flow diverts away from the digestive tract.

Immune function: lower resistance to illness and longer recovery from infections

Memory & cognition: difficulty concentrating, fragmented memory, and brain fog

Memory also stores trauma: muscles may remain tense long after danger has passed, digestion may remain unsettled, and the heart may race at the slightest cue. These physical patterns reflect the body's attempt to survive, even when the threat is no longer present.

Many survivors describe feeling as though their bodies remember the abuse in ways the mind cannot explain. Headaches, chronic pain, autoimmune conditions, and cardiovascular issues are all more common among people who have lived under prolonged coercive control. These are not signs of weakness, but of a body that has been working too hard, for too long, to keep someone safe.

## From the Therapy Room

I have worked with people whose partners or family members controlled every dollar, tracked every message, and slowly cut them off from friends, colleagues, and community. Others even dictated some people's ability to leave their houses on remote properties. Some survivors shared how their partners insisted on bringing home all the food each day, strictly rationed into small portions. They described being so hungry that they would hide scraps or secretly eat whatever they could find to get through.

This kind of control does not fade when the relationship ends. It can carve deep marks not only on the heart but on the body itself. Years later, survivors have shared how they needed to collaborate with dietitians and therapists to relearn something as basic as eating regularly, to rebuild trust in food, and to quiet the guilt or fear that rose with every meal.

## My journey

In my life, the impact of coercive control has not only been emotional but intensely physical. After years of stress and trauma, my body broke down in ways I could not ignore. I required an emergency hysterectomy after heavy bleeding, and two years later, I still carry the bruises on my arms. My ongoing stomach problems, a low immune system, and even struggles with food remind me that trauma does not just live in memories; it can live in the body.

Even now, I can slip back into old eating issues when stress rises; a reminder of how control and fear can shape everyday life, even years later. Healing my emotional wounds has helped me see this more clearly: the severity of my health issues was not random, but a reflection of how deeply domestic violence had taken root in my body.

Therefore, recognising coercive control matters so much. Without understanding its full impact, people might assume the damage ends when the relationship does. But the marks of coercive control can remain long after in the cells of the very body that carried us through survival.

## Research Insight

What I describe as the 9 Masks of Coercive Control reflects patterns consistently identified in research and practice. Stark (2007) highlights isolation, surveillance, and micro-regulation as core pillars of coercive control. Kelly and Westmorland (2016) also show that policy responses often minimise or downplay these behaviours.

Work on abusive dynamics emphasises recurring cycles: Bancroft (2002) and Stosny (1995) describe the grooming pattern of charm, pity plays, and emotional manipulation. These often coexist with ongoing criticism and contempt; themes echoed in Walker's (2017) work on battered women's syndrome and Herman's (1992/2015) research on trauma.

Other scholars have identified specific tactics. Sweet (2019) and Sarkis (2018) analyse gaslighting as a systematic strategy of distortion, while Katz (2016) demonstrates how children both suffer under, and actively resist, regimes of surveillance. Douglas and

Burdon (2018) highlight the modern dimension of technology-facilitated abuse. Dobash and Dobash (2004) identify intimidation and threats as central to the concept of coercive control. Finally, Mahoney (1991) shows how legal and social systems can themselves entrap survivors, reinforcing Stark's conclusion that the aim of coercive control is not merely harm, but entrapment.

## Self-Reflection: Spotting the Patterns

Take a few minutes to notice where coercive control might show up in your own life, someone you care about, or even the relationships you see in your professional work.

Are there areas where your choices feel restricted, such as what you wear, who you see, or what you spend?

Do you often feel afraid to speak up or worried about upsetting someone?

Have you slowly stopped seeing friends, family, or doing things you used to enjoy?

Do you explain or justify every choice, even small ones?

There are no right or wrong answers; this is just about becoming aware. The first step to regaining freedom is recognising the invisible chains.

# Neuroscience and Perpetrator Behaviour

This chapter takes a neurological lens to perpetrator behaviour. It offers no excuses, but sheds light on how brain function can interact with coercive control, abuse and the cycle of violence. By exploring the science, we can see patterns more clearly, respond more effectively, and support interventions that aim for meaningful and lasting change. Experiences, especially traumatic ones, can alter our thoughts, emotions, and behaviour.

My work with both survivors and perpetrators of domestic abuse has only deepened that curiosity. Understanding what happens in the brain does not excuse harmful behaviour, but it can help us understand why coercive control can feel so hard to escape. It can also explain why some perpetrators continue to repeat destructive patterns, even when expressing a desire to change.

When discussing behaviour, people often revive the nature versus nurture debate. This concept raises the discussion of whether people are born this way or if life experiences shape who they become. Most parents will tell you that even children raised under the same roof can be chalk and cheese: one calm and empathetic, while the other is impulsive or reactive. Neuroscience shows the truth lies somewhere in between. Biology creates certain tendencies, but environment, relationships, and trauma can amplify or soften them.

## Psychological and Neurological Drivers

Research in neurocriminology and psychology shows that many perpetrators of coercive control display differences in three key areas: empathy, impulse regulation, and threat response. Neuroimaging studies reveal changes in parts of the brain, such as.

Decision-making and impulse control are in the prefrontal cortex.

The amygdala plays a crucial role in fear processing and reactivity.

Emotional regulation is associated with the anterior cingulate cortex.

These findings help explain that when the victim tries to leave or assert independence, it is often the most dangerous time. A perpetrator's brain can process losing control as a direct threat, which sparks escalation.

However, brain differences do not excuse harm. Thanks to neuroplasticity, the brain can form new pathways. With insight, accountability, and consistent intervention, harmful patterns can shift. People need to choose to change and practice it, rather than being coerced or having it imposed upon them.


## Understanding the Neurological Lens

Neurocriminology research highlights three recurring patterns often observed in people who use coercive control or domestic abuse. These patterns do not excuse harmful behaviour, but they help explain how abusive cycles persist.

### Disrupted Impulse Control
Difficulty regulating anger or frustration, leading to coercion, threats, or violence.

Example: Explosive reactions to small triggers, such as shouting, breaking objects, or making threats, followed by a calm period that resets the cycle.

**Distorted Reasoning**
Thinking patterns that excuse, minimise, or justify abusive behaviour.
Example: blaming the victim, twisting facts, or reframing control as care or protection.

**Lack of Empathy**
Inability or unwillingness to recognise the victim's feelings, needs, or suffering.
Example: Dismissing distress, mocking emotions, or ignoring obvious harm caused.

**Interaction of Neurological Patterns**

Reduced empathy can make it easier for someone with poor impulse control to lash out without remorse.

Neuroscience shows that many perpetrators of domestic abuse display deficits in executive functioning, planning, impulse inhibition, and working memory linked to prefrontal cortex activity. Impaired moral reasoning and moral disengagement then allow the abuser to reframe the harm as justified.

Research has found:

Structural differences, such as reduced grey matter in the prefrontal and orbitofrontal cortices (areas involved in impulse control and moral decision-making), have been associated with violent behaviour.

Researchers have linked head injuries to increased moral disengagement and poorer behavioural regulation.

Neuroimaging studies showing reduced activation in brain regions support empathy deficits tied to emotional recognition and processing.

Together, these factors can form self-reinforcing loops. Each incident of abuse strengthens the neural pathways involved in threat response and aggression, making future outbursts more likely and automatic. This helps explain why coercive control can become so entrenched.

## Autism, Personality, and Domestic Violence

When we talk about the psychology or neurology of coercive control, it is essential to avoid confusion and stigma. Two conditions often raised in public conversation are autism and narcissistic personality disorder (NPD), but the research tells two quite different stories.

### Autism and DV

People on the autism spectrum are not more likely to be perpetrators of domestic violence.

In fact, studies show they are more likely to be victims/survivors, facing higher rates of coercion, exploitation, and abuse.

Others may sometimes misunderstand traits such as difficulty reading social cues, but these differ from abuse.

## Narcissistic Personality Disorder and DV

Research consistently shows that narcissistic traits such as entitlement, lack of empathy, and a need for control contribute to higher rates of intimate partner violence.

Coercive control and NPD can overlap; both may involve blame-shifting, gaslighting, and domination.

A diagnosis alone does not make someone abusive. Abuse is always about choices, responsibility, and power, not simply about personality labels.

## Why This Matters?

Autism, ADHD, depression, or other neurodivergence does not cause domestic and family violence. It is most strongly associated with power, entitlement, and control, sometimes reinforced by personality traits such as those found in NPD or antisocial patterns. By separating myth from evidence, we protect people from stigma and hold perpetrators accountable for their behaviour.

## Distinguishing Neuroscience from Character Traits

Neuroscience examines the brain's biological foundations, including neural circuits, neurotransmitters, and the networks that shape our responses to the world. Character traits are what we can observe from the outside: attitudes, behaviours, and personality patterns. The two overlap, but they are not the same.

For example, someone described as having low empathy may also show reduced activation in brain regions involved in emotional recognition and processing. However, life experience, trauma, and culture also shape empathy.

A history of attachment wounds, chronic stress, or exposure to violence can blunt or heighten empathic responses. What we see in behaviour is therefore a mix of biology and environment.

Understanding this distinction matters. If we focus only on character, we risk moralising behaviour as simply good or bad. If we focus only on neuroscience, we risk excusing it as biologically inevitable. The truth lies somewhere in between: biology creates tendencies, but experience, accountability, and intervention shape what happens next.

Practical Example
Imagine two people who both display explosive anger:

**Person A** - exhibits reduced activation in the prefrontal cortex and struggles to inhibit impulses.

**Person B** - learned aggression through childhood modelling but shows normal brain regulation.

From the outside, they look similar. However, their treatment needs differ. Person A may benefit most from therapies that strengthen regulation (e.g., CBT, mindfulness, biofeedback). Person B may benefit more from psychoeducation, healthy role-modelling, and conflict resolution skills.

Therefore, looking beneath the surface matters. The behaviour of these two individuals may appear the same on the surface. However, the underlying pathways are not always identical; therefore, the supports that help change stick are also divergent.

Current behaviour changes often lead to programs applying one framework for all, focusing rightly on accountability and responsibility. Neuroscience reminds us that some individuals may also require targeted support besides these programs to address issues related to regulation, empathy, or trauma. Without this, the risk of relapse or superficial change remains high.

## The Brain and Behaviour

The human brain exhibits plasticity, meaning it constantly adapts and changes in response to experience. Therefore, coercive control can become more entrenched the longer it continues, but encouragingly, this is also why change is possible.

Several factors shape how change happens:

Age and Development: Younger brains are more flexible and adapt more quickly. Adults can also change, but it usually requires more time, effort, and consistent practice.

Consistency and repetition: new, healthier patterns need to be practised again until they replace old habits and become the brain's default setting.

Emotional engagement: Actual change happens when a person feels genuine motivation and can connect with

empathy, responsibility, and accountability for the harm they have caused.

Therapeutic programs that combine the elements of repetition, emotional awareness, and personal responsibility offer the best chance of breaking entrenched cycles of harmful behaviour.

## The Impact of Drugs, Alcohol, and Addiction on the Brain

Substance use can significantly alter brain function, particularly in regions associated with decision-making, impulse control, and emotional regulation.

Prefrontal Cortex Impairment: Alcohol and many drugs temporarily suppress activity in the brain's braking system. Over time, heavy use can cause structural changes that reduce regulation even when sober.

Reward System Hijacking: Addictions, whether to substances, gambling, pornography, or even compulsive gaming, hijack dopamine pathways, leading the brain to prioritise the addictive behaviour over healthy coping, relationships, and long-term goals.

Increased Reactivity: Some substances, particularly stimulants, methamphetamine, and cocaine, heighten amygdala activation, making people more reactive, paranoid, or aggressive.

Addiction often intensifies the cycle of abuse: poor impulse control leads to harm, shame fuels further substance use, and the neural pathways of aggression and avoidance grow stronger.

## Neuroplasticity and Addiction

The hopeful news is that the brain can rewire after substance misuse; however, it takes time, consistency, and support. The brain needs to recalibrate dopamine pathways, and people must practice new habits repeatedly until the brain defaults to them.

Early Abstinence: In the first weeks and months of sobriety, the brain may feel "foggy" or depleted as it adjusts to lower dopamine stimulation. Cravings, irritability, anxiety, and sleep disruption are common during this stage. Because the nervous system is recalibrating, doctors often need to monitor the patient to ensure safety.

Six to twelve months: With sustained abstinence or behaviour change, brain function recovers. Research shows measurable improvements in the prefrontal cortex (responsible for planning and impulse control), as well as in memory, emotional regulation, and decision-making.

Support is Critical: Addiction is not just a chemical process, but a behavioural and relational one as well. Co-dependency can form when survival patterns such as caretaking, people-pleasing, or enabling become deeply ingrained. Structured therapy, peer groups, and safe support systems are crucial for reinforcing new pathways, reducing the risk of relapse, and supporting both the individual and those around them.

Recovery is possible, but the process is rarely linear. Understanding the brain's healing process helps explain why compassion, structure, and monitoring are vital during withdrawal and early sobriety.

## Intergenerational Trauma and the Brain

Coercive control does not just harm the person living through it in the present. It can leave a biological imprint that is passed down to future generations.

Research in neuroscience and epigenetics shows that long-term stress and trauma can change how the body's stress-response system works. One key system is the hypothalamic-pituitary-adrenal (HPA) axis, which enables us to respond to danger by releasing stress hormones, such as cortisol. When someone lives in constant fear, this system can become overactive or shut down, making it harder to regulate emotions or feel safe.

Trauma, research in epigenetics also suggests, can influence which parts of our DNA switch on or off. This does not alter the genetic code itself, but it can affect gene expression.

For children growing up with coercive control, this can mean:

Heightened stress responses, being on edge or quick to react, even in safe situations.

Difficulty regulating emotions, struggling to calm down after upset or stress.

Increased vulnerability to anxiety, depression, or health problems later in life.

Learning patterns of fear and control as usual, which can affect future relationships.

This science helps explain why coercive control, a private issue between adults, is not just restricted to them. Still, it can also shape the biological, emotional, and social well-being of the next generation.

**Hyperactive Stress Systems**

Children's brains may become wired for danger, making them extra sensitive to threat and more vulnerable to anxiety, depression, or PTSD later in life.

**Emotional Regulation Challenges**

Underdeveloped brain systems for calming and regulation mean it is harder to settle once triggered. This can lead to explosive outbursts or, at the other extreme, complete shutdown and withdrawal.

**Risk of Repetition**

Without support, children may absorb unhealthy relationship models. This leaves them more vulnerable to either using control or becoming targets of it in adulthood.

Breaking the cycle requires more than simply removing a child from harm. Healing comes through therapy, safe caregiving relationships, and repeated experiences of co-regulation. A calm adult can help the child's nervous system feel secure enough to rest. Over time, these experiences rewire the stress system towards balance.

**Epigenetics and Trauma**

Scientists know now that trauma shapes our feelings and memories. This field of research is called epigenetics.

Here is the simple version:

Our DNA is like a library; all the genes are there.

Epigenetics decides which books are open and which are closed.

Chronic stress, fear, or abuse can switch on genes that heighten stress responses (like cortisol production) and switch off genes that help with calming and repair.

The next generation can even inherit some of these changes. A parent's experience of trauma can shape how their child's stress system develops even before birth.

The hopeful part is that epigenetic changes are not permanent. With safety, therapy, and nurturing relationships, the body can reopen healthy books in the library and quieten the ones that keep people stuck in a state of survival mode.

Therefore, breaking the cycle of coercive control matters. It is not only about ending harm today but also about giving the next generation the chance to grow up with calmer, healthier stress control systems.

## The Future of Neuroscience and Coercive Control

Neuroscience is rapidly advancing, and its role in understanding violence, coercive control, and criminal behaviour is still in its early stages. We know only a small amount of what will be possible in the future.

Researchers are exploring questions such as

Brain-Based Risk Profiling
Could neuroimaging one day help identify individuals at high risk of escalating violence before harm occurs? While still theoretical, early studies on brain activity patterns suggest it may be possible to map circuits associated with impulse control, empathy, and aggression.

Personalised Interventions
If clinicians could identify which brain systems are underactive or overactive (for example, empathy networks or regions involved in impulse control),

treatment could become more tailored. This could mean faster, more effective interventions that target the specific neural pathways involved.

Ethical Dilemmas
As neuroscience advances, profound ethical questions arise:
Should courts allow brain scans as evidence to explain or mitigate responsibility? Could neuroscience one day influence custody decisions, sentencing, or mandated treatment? If so, how do we ensure this does not unintentionally excuse harmful behaviour or undermine accountability?

.

## From the Therapy Room

Over the years, I have seen how similar behaviours on the surface can mask very different drivers underneath. Neuroscience helps us look beneath those behaviours to understand the brain processes that fuel them. These insights can shape interventions and improve outcomes.

I once worked with a caregiver, and someone reported them for intimidation and property damage during parenting exchanges. They had a long history of alcohol misuse. Alcohol had reshaped their brains' functioning in three simple ways:

Impulse control weakened: years of drinking impaired the prefrontal cortex, the brain's braking system, making it harder to pause before reacting.

Reward pathways hijacked: Under stress, the brain priorities immediate relief, such as drinking, shouting, slamming doors, over long-term consequences, the impact on children, court orders, or safety.

Heightened threat response: The amygdala, the brain's alarm system, was overactive, triggering anger and defensiveness even at minor frustrations.

With support and accountability, this person saw how alcohol was fuelling their behaviour. Pairing sobriety with regulation strategies slowly disrupted old patterns. Similar dynamics often appear with behavioural addictions such as gambling or compulsive gaming. Outwardly, it may look like just anger issues, but neuroscience reveals how substance use and addictions can entrench cycles of coercive control.

In another case, two people went into the same behaviour-change program. On paper, their behaviour looked almost identical: shouting, intimidation, and anger in the home. Both initially denied responsibility. However, as the weeks unfolded, the differences became apparent:

The impulsive reactor: Anger flared instantly over minor frustrations, followed by genuine shock at how quickly things had escalated. Neuropsychologically, this reflected deficits in regulation: their prefrontal cortex struggled to apply the brakes. Once they added mindfulness and grounding to the program, they noticed triggers earlier and practised pausing before reacting.

The calculated controller: Their outbursts were deliberate and strategic, often planned to "teach a lesson." The issue was not regulation but belief systems, entitlement, distorted reasoning, and moral disengagement. Their intervention needed to focus on accountability and confronting those beliefs, rather than just addressing anger management.

I also worked with a parent who repeatedly disobeyed parenting orders. Psychological testing showed poor impulse control and high emotional reactivity. Family members described a pattern of coercive control: monitoring phone calls, interfering with school attendance, and threatening to withhold money.

After the separation, the behaviour escalated, with frequent unannounced visits, constant messaging, and attempts to turn the children against the other caregiver. Neuroscience helps us understand why people can experience separation as a profound loss of control, which over-activates the amygdala and stress-response systems. The result is hypervigilant, defensive, and often retaliatory behaviour.

With intensive intervention — weekly therapy focused on regulation, group behaviour-change sessions, and close court oversight — this parent gradually recognised their triggers. They practised pausing before reacting, reframing thoughts that justified harm, and finding healthier coping strategies. Over time, incidents of aggression decreased, and the children reported feeling safer.

These experiences reinforced two lessons that research also highlights:

People must plan for risk escalation after separation, where coercive control and family and domestic violence exist.

Targeted neurological and behavioural interventions can work, but only when combined with accountability and consistent monitoring.

## Research Insight

Neuroscience research helps explain why coercive control can feel so deeply entrenched, while also showing that change remains possible. Studies link dysfunction in the prefrontal cortex—particularly the ventromedial and orbitofrontal regions—to impaired moral decision-making and impulse regulation, which increases vulnerability to aggression and antisocial behaviour (Blair, 2013; Raine, 2013). Empathy relies on brain circuits, including the anterior insula and anterior cingulate cortex. However, neuroimaging reveals that individuals with high psychopathic traits often display reduced activation in these regions when imagining others in pain, suggesting a blunted recognition of suffering (Decety, Chen, Harenski, & Kiehl, 2013). Addiction research further shows how alcohol and substance use disorders hijack reward and stress circuits, particularly within the extended amygdala, while weakening prefrontal regulation, making relapse and harmful behaviours more likely under stress (Koob & Volkow, 2016). Importantly, change is possible: longitudinal MRI studies show recovery of cortical thickness in frontal regions after sustained abstinence from alcohol, underscoring the brain's capacity for neuroplasticity and repair with consistent practice, accountability, and support (Zahr & Pfefferbaum, 2017; Durazzo, Stephens, & Meyerhoff, 2023). These findings together highlight the dual reality of coercive control—its deep neurological roots, but also the potential for recovery when safe, structured, and supportive ways to address the behaviour.

## Important points

Addiction amplifies neurological vulnerabilities, making it harder to regulate behaviour and easier to stay trapped in coercive cycles.

Motivation and engagement matter; actual change only occurs when the person is willing to do the hard work of rewiring their brain through sobriety and repeated practices of change.

Early intervention promotes neuroplasticity. Addressing substance use or behavioural addictions sooner increases the likelihood of reshaping brain pathways and stabilising behaviour.

**Gentle Note:** Understanding the brain does not mean excusing abuse. Neuroscience can help us know how harmful patterns develop, but it never removes the responsibility for choosing those patterns. Every person has a choice in how they treat others.

Perpetrators may need different support to shift their behaviour, but accountability always comes first. Abuse is never solely biological, nor is it simply a product of upbringing.

It is a decision to use power and control, and it is always the responsibility of the person causing harm to stop.

# The pattern of coercive control

## The Cycle of Violence

For many years, the cycle of violence has been used to explain patterns of abuse. It describes how relationships can move through recurring phases:

Tension Building: stress rises, minor arguments occur, and the victim feels as though they are walking on eggshells.

Explosions: verbal, physical, or psychological violence erupts.

Honeymoon Phase: the perpetrator apologises, promises change, or shows affection, giving hope that things will improve.

This model was also important for demonstrating that abuse is a pattern, not an isolated incident. However, it focuses mainly on incidents of violence. This does not fully capture the constant, everyday control that defines many abusive relationships.

## Beyond Incidents: The Invisible Web

This is where the concept of coercive control changes our understanding. Unlike the cycle of violence, coercive control is not about isolated events or occasional explosions; it is an ongoing system of domination, woven through daily life.

People often refer to coercive control as a liberty crime because it aims to strip away a person's freedom, autonomy, and sense of self. At first, the behaviours may look small, even disguised as care, for example:

'I worry when you go out without me.'

However, over time, these behaviours accumulate, closing in like invisible chains. Survivors describe feeling monitored, restricted, and trapped even when no visible violence has occurred.

## Why This Shift Matters?

Understanding coercive control as an invisible web helps explain why leaving can feel like an impossible task. While the Cycle of Violence highlights repetition and escalation, coercive control shows us how abuse can infiltrate every corner of life. This can involve finances, friendships, identity, freedom of movement, and even thought.

By examining both models, we can gain a comprehensive view.

Cycles of violence remind us that abuse is rarely a one-off event.

Coercive control reveals the deeper system that sustains it every day.

## Impact Isolation: Shrinking the World

Isolation is one of the most powerful tactics. By cutting off supports, perpetrators remove outside perspectives and deepen dependence.

How It Can Play Out:

'You don't need to work; I want to look after you ' someone promised a partner, financial security to persuade them to quit their job, saying they do not need the money. Later, they find themselves financially entrapped.

Social invitations get intercepted with the message, 'Oh, I forgot to tell you, we already had plans that night.' "aww but I really wanted us to just have time together" or 'Every time your family comes over, they cause problems and are jealous of us; they are trying to break us up' Over time, this can make visitors feel unwelcome or lead to punishment afterwards, such as the silent treatment, slammed doors, or banging objects until submission. To avoid the drama, the survivor declines invitations or stops having people over.

Hiding car keys, cancelling plans, or insisting on a move to a house for a fresh start often leads to a rural or isolated area.

Car tyres mysteriously go flat, or there are sudden car issues that are later miraculously fixed when the perpetrator needs the car.

Unexpectedly showing up at work to have lunch together, framed as love or care, but preventing the survivor from forming social bonds with colleagues.

Impact

Isolation fuels anxiety and depression. Neuroscience reveals that it overactivates the stress response, including cortisol and the amygdala, which can make memory and problem-solving more challenging.

Practical tip

Stay in touch with at least one trusted person. If face-to-face contact is not safe, try anonymous helplines, online forums, or DV services.

## Monitoring and Surveillance: Living Under Watch

The documentation of technology-facilitated abuse is now extensive. Surveillance is not about love or safety, but control. It creates a constant sense of being watched, which erodes autonomy and heightens fear.

This can include:

Demanding passwords for trust, then checking phones, emails, or bank accounts. A survivor discovers their partner has been reviewing their phone records through a shared account and confronts them about every call. Over time, they stop calling friends altogether.

Driving past home or work to check in or unexpectedly showing up at work to have lunch. What appears to be care can prevent the survivor from building social connections and make them feel monitored.

Installing cameras or smart-home devices under the guise of security. These tools are used to track movements, control the environment (lights, heating, locks), and even make the home feel unsafe.

Using shared phone plans or hidden apps to track movements. A survivor finds a safety app secretly installed on their device. Soon, every unexplained five-minute delay results in interrogation or accusations.

Constant surveillance traps the nervous system in a state of hypervigilance. Prolonged arousal disrupts memory, decision-making, and sleep, while leaving the survivor feeling as though there is no private space left to think, act, or even breathe.

If safe, turn off location sharing on devices and review privacy settings. Seek support from tech-safety organisations that specialise in countering digital abuse. Develop a safety plan before making significant changes, as perpetrators often escalate when someone interferes with their control and monitoring.

Some perpetrators will question their victims about their movements after monitoring them all day via location. If they miss reporting something or do not share every detail. The perpetrators accuse the victims of lying and tell them the victims are not trustworthy.

It can then justify the perpetrator's behaviour because it makes it your fault for not being honest.

## JADE: The Trap of Justifying and Explaining

JADE stands for Justify, Argue, Defend, and Explain. Perpetrators use this cycle to exhaust, confuse, and weaken survivors. Instead of resolving conflict, it traps the survivor in endless debates where they feel pressured to prove themselves. While not a clinical term, advocates and therapists widely recognise JADE as a key communication trap in coercive control.

How It Can Play Out

'So now I cannot even raise my voice? You are controlling me!'

'After everything I have done for you, you still complain?'

'If you really loved me and trusted me, you would not question me.'

A survivor argues until 3 am, desperately trying to defend their choices. Exhausted, they give in to end the fight.

The abuser twists every attempt by the survivor to set a boundary into counterarguments until the survivor feels confused or at fault.

Over time, the survivor stops raising concerns altogether, believing silence is safer.

Impact
The JADE cycle keeps the nervous system locked in a state of fight-or-flight. It erodes confidence, blurs truth, and deepens trauma bonds. Survivors often describe feeling mentally drained, silenced, and unable to trust their own perspective.

Practical tip
Boundaries do not need debate; your feelings and needs also matter. If you feel drawn to defending yourself, try a simple, neutral response, such as, 'I will not argue about this.' Please step away from circular conversations rather than trying to win them.

## Gaslighting: Losing Your Sense of Reality

Gaslighting is a form of psychological abuse that makes someone doubt their memory, perception, or sanity. Over time, this dependency shifts power to the perpetrator, whose version of events becomes the only truth.

How It Can Play Out

'It never happened; you are imagining things.'

'You are too sensitive. It was just a joke.'

'I never said that. You must be confused.'

Someone deliberately moves household items, then tells the survivor they are losing it.

A survivor notices missing money from a joint account, but their partner insists they must have forgotten about the purchase. Some have doctored bank statements by filtering to make the survivor question their reality.

The perpetrator convinces the victim that they are mentally well.

Impact

Gaslighting undermines the brain's memory systems, particularly the hippocampus, leaving survivors confused, anxious, and increasingly dependent. Many victims report having depression, self-doubt, lack of confidence and sometimes leading to a diagnosis of posttraumatic stress disorder or complex posttraumatic stress disorder.

Practical tip

Keep a written or photo record of events (where safe). Share observations with a trusted friend, therapist, or support worker to reality-check your experiences and rebuild confidence in your memory and perception. Some victims emailed the information to a hidden address or stored it on a hidden memory stick for future use.

**Threats, Intimidation, and Conditional Kindness**

Perpetrators often combine threats with periods of affection or honeymoon phases. This intermittent reinforcement strengthens trauma bonds, making it harder for survivors to leave.

How It Can Play Out

'If you leave, you will never see the kids again.' 'The kids will hate you for splitting up the family'

Smashing objects, harming pets, or threatening self-harm to prevent separation.

Someone screams at a survivor one night, then gives the survivor flowers, breakfast in bed, and massages the next day.

A partner smashes a phone during an argument, then spends days being "extra kind."

In public, the perpetrator charms and shows affection, which makes the survivor feel lucky. At home, the perpetrator punishes the same victim with silence for supposedly looking at another person or embarrassing them in front of others.

Expensive gifts, grand gestures, cars, holidays — yet often used against you later to justify behaviour. If I didn't love you, then why would I buy you all these things? You make me act the way I do sometimes

Threats, intimidation, and apologies pull at the nervous system, activating dopamine and stress circuits, reinforcing the trauma bond and making escape difficult. This push-pull activates dopamine and stress circuits, reinforcing the trauma bond and making escape even harder.

Practical Tip
Recognise the honeymoon kindness as part of the cycle, not proof of actual change. If threats escalate, seek urgent crisis support and work with a domestic violence service to plan for safety.

## Financial Abuse

Financial abuse is one of the most common and devastating forms of coercive control. It limits independence, creates dependency, and often leaves survivors without the resources to leave.

How It Can Play Out

'I will handle the money — you are bad with finances.'

Taking wages or forcing someone to beg for their basic needs.

Blocking access to work or study opportunities.

Creating debt in another person's name.

A survivor wants to study part-time, but the perpetrator refuses, claiming money is too tight while freely spending on personal hobbies. The perpetrator leaves the survivor begging for essentials.

Impact
Financial control traps survivors in dependency. It creates chronic stress, impairs the brain's planning and problem-solving, and reinforces the belief that leaving is impossible.

Practical Tip
If safe, open a private bank account and store copies of key financial documents in a secure location. Seek advice from a financial counsellor or support service to explore options.

## Why These Patterns Are So Powerful

Individually, these behaviours might look small, even excusable. Together, they form a system of domination, one that traps survivors emotionally, financially, psychologically, and legally.

## Recognising the Patterns of Coercive Control

No One-Size Perpetrator

Not every perpetrator uses the same tactics. Some rely more on intimidation, while others use surveillance or financial leverage. What matters is the pattern.

Care or control.

Early behaviour can look like love:

Checking in constantly.

Wanting to spend all their time together.

Handling money "to help."

Later, these may escalate into monitoring, isolation, and financial control.

Survivors often see the pattern only in hindsight. Each restriction feels minor or excusable. Step by step, the net tightens.

**Someone personalises control.**

They tailor tactics to a person's vulnerabilities, which can include

Immigration status, threats of deportation.

Parenting role using children as leverage.

Housing insecurity.

Disability or illness restricting medication, appointments, or care.

Coming from a family where their own parents separated.

Not being good enough for anyone else.
Indoctrination that the victim needs the perpetrator to survive as they would not survive alone

## Cycles can look the same, but drivers differ.

Some perpetrators act impulsively; others plan. Although the behaviours seem similar, the underlying drivers are different.

## Kindness in Intervals: The Power Within

The cycle of cruelty confuses the brain's reward system and the sudden affection honeymoon phase. Hope keeps survivors hooked, even when fear is a constant presence.

Key Insight:

Coercive control is less about any one act and more about the pattern. Coercive control does not always take the same form. The tactics may differ, but the aim is always the same: to dominate and restrict another person's freedom.

## From My journey

Living under coercive control for so long has distorted my sense of what love looks like. What I once thought was love, I have since learned was often a tactic of control. Even now, I still catch myself questioning:

Someone cutting up my food for me ...is that kindness, or is it about power?

An app to see where I am... is that protection, or surveillance?

Constant calls and texts checking in... is that care or monitoring?

Being told what to wear is not sweet... or is it control?

One day, someone treated me like a princess; the next, someone ignored me, with no idea what I had done.

Receiving extravagant gifts with one hand, only to have something taken with the other.

As a child, someone conditioned me to believe I was property. As an adult, someone taught me that love meant dependence under control.

Therefore, coercive control is so powerful and so confusing. What is normal, safe, and loving? Even after leaving, those beliefs can linger. I have remained single for now because I am still unlearning these patterns, rebuilding, and trying to understand what healthy love feels like. Part of that is learning to trust my judgment again in relationships.

Who knows, one day I will create a list of selection criteria for applicants. Through it all, I have a great sense of humour. Life is too short not to laugh, even in the middle of rebuilding.

# Coercive Control Beyond the Intimate Partner

## Coercive Control in Friendships

When people think of coercive control, they often imagine intimate partner violence. However, coercion also occurs outside of romantic relationships. It can also emerge in friendships — spaces where trust, loyalty, and a sense of belonging provide a sense of safety. A controlling friend may present themselves as protective or devoted, but beneath the surface lies a pattern of dominance that erodes autonomy. Over time, what starts as closeness can become entrapment, where guilt, fear of abandonment, and manipulation replace genuine connection.

Friendship coercion is often overlooked because it masquerades as loyalty. Survivors may dismiss the behaviour as "clinginess" or "over-protectiveness." However, when a friend consistently isolates, undermines, or manipulates, the impact mirrors other coercive dynamics: the survivor loses their freedom to choose, doubts their own judgment, and becomes increasingly dependent on the controlling friend.

How It Appears

**Isolation:** monopolising time and discouraging other friendships.

**Secrets and debts**: using shared confidences or past favours to bind loyalty.

**Jealousy** framed as loyalty: guilt-tripping over outside connections.

**Conditional support** means withdrawing warmth or care when someone does not meet expectations or sets a boundary.

**Surveillance:** monitoring social media, questioning who the survivor spends time with, or demanding constant updates.

Example 1: Guilt and Withdrawal
A person reconnects with old friends. Their best friend responds: "I guess I am not good enough anymore."

Overwhelmed with guilt, they withdraw again, becoming increasingly dependent on one controlling friend.

Example 2: Secrets as Leverage
Two friends share intimate secrets during a vulnerable time. Later, one says, "Do not forget who knows everything about you. You would not want that getting out." Fear of exposure silences the person and binds them to the relationship, even when it feels unsafe.

Example 3: Jealousy as Proof of Loyalty
Someone tells a close friend that they plan to spend the weekend with others. The friend snaps: "After everything I have done for you, you are ditching me?" The guilt is so intense that they cancel their plans, learning that loyalty requires sacrificing other relationships.

Control in friendships often becomes visible when one person seeks connection outside the friendship, whether through dating, family ties, or new acquaintances. The controlling friend may:

Manipulate other friendships by spreading rumours, creating conflict, or questioning the motives of new friends ("They do not really care about you — they are just using you").

React with jealousy when the friend dates someone new, framing it as a proof of disloyalty ("Now that you are with them, you do not care about me anymore").

Use guilt or ultimatums to monopolise time ("If you really cared, you would cancel your plans with them and be with me").

These tactics mirror coercive control in intimate partner dynamics. Where a partner may restrict contact with friends or monitor social life to maintain dominance, a controlling friend weaponises loyalty and belonging. The result is the same: erosion of autonomy, isolation from broader support networks, and dependency on the controlling relationship.

A question to ask yourself about your friendships is, are you scared to tell them something you are planning or going to be doing because they will make an issue out of it and make you feel you're going against them or the friendship?

### Research insight:

According to Kraft & Mayeux (2018), friendship jealousy predicts relational aggression behaviours such as exclusion, manipulation, and undermining a friend's social connections. These tactics reflect the patterns of coercive control, which exploits emotional bonds and social belonging to isolate and dominate, making the targeted person dependent and disempowered.

## Coercive Control in Society

Coercive control appears not only in personal relationships. Laws, institutions, and cultural narratives can also weave it into the fabric of society. When systems use power to silence, restrict, or punish certain groups under the guise of "order" or "protection," the impact can mirror the same entrapment seen in interpersonal dynamics. Survivors of family and domestic violence often describe not only being controlled by a partner but also being re-traumatised by social systems that replicate the same patterns of dominance.

## Child Support and Wage Garnishment

How it works: If a parent falls behind on child support, agencies may garnish wages, intercept tax returns, or suspend licences.

Where it becomes coercive control, it strips the individual of autonomy and dignity, creating dependency on the system while threatening livelihood.

Parallel to coercive control, much like an abuser withholding or controlling finances, the system enforces

compliance through financial surveillance and punishment, often leaving the person fearful and trapped.

## Child Protection and Contact Decisions

How it works: Child protection agencies sometimes issue directives or court orders that restrict a parent's contact with their children.

When decisions lack transparency or when protective parents face threats of child removal for reporting violence, the system employs fear and isolation to ensure obedience.

Parallels to coercive control: This mirrors how perpetrators isolate survivors from their children or weaponised fear of separation to maintain control.

### Welfare Conditionality

The system operates by enforcing strict compliance requirements, including reporting, job applications, and program attendance, as well as social security payments.

When it becomes coercive control, with minor breaches triggering disproportionate sanctions — such as losing all payments — it creates dependency and entrapment.

Parallel to coercive control: Like a partner threatening abandonment or withdrawal of resources, the system enforces obedience through the constant threat of financial punishment.

### Family Court Processes

How it works: Survivors of coercive control often rely on courts for protection or parenting arrangements.

Where it becomes coercive control, courts may minimise coercive control as "mutual conflict" or compel contact between a child and an abusive parent. Survivors are often explicitly warned that they must not share details of proceedings outside the court, even when doing so might bring them support or advocacy. This enforced silence, combined with the risk of punishment for resistance, mirrors the tactics of coercive control. Survivors find others denying their reality, constraining their voice, and stripping their autonomy. Parallel to coercive control, just as perpetrators gaslight, isolate, and forbid survivors from speaking out, legal processes can replicate the same silencing by restricting disclosure and enforcing compliance. The result is a system that unintentionally reinforces the very dynamics it seeks to dismantle.

## Workplace Surveillance

How it works: increasing use of monitoring software, tracking keystrokes, cameras, or time-logging in workplaces.

In a coercive control setting, those in the workplace lose their sense of agency and self-trust when others micromanage, constantly monitor and penalise them for minor lapses.

Parallels to coercive control: exactly like domestic coercive control, where surveillance and monitoring maintain dominance.

## Research insight

Evan Stark (2007) defines coercive control as a "liberty crime" — a patterned regime of domination that strips autonomy and entraps a person in everyday life. Though he analysed intimate partner violence, later scholars extended this view, and they showed how state and institutional structures can also replicate coercive dynamics.

Welfare conditionality research shows that benefits systems enforce compliance through the threat of financial sanction, mirroring abusers' use of financial control to secure obedience (Dwyer et al., 2018).

Higher education studies reveal how institutions may rely on hidden pressures, intimidation, and dependency, creating a model of coercive control within academic life (Jakovljevic et al., 2022).

Earlier, Goroff (1974) argued that social welfare operates as "coercive social control", embedding behavioural rules into policy frameworks that punish non-compliance.

Unlike some countries, Australia does not have a general constitutional right to freedom of speech. The High Court has only recognised implied freedom of political communication (Australian Capital Television v Commonwealth, 1992; Lange v ABC, 1997). This protects public debate about government, but not personal disclosures about family violence. Even this interpretation is short, although the Constitution explicitly refers to freedom of religion in s 116. This means perpetrators can

Silence survivors of family violence twice: first, they forbid disclosure, and second, legal systems criminalise sharing proceedings outside the courtroom (Family Law Act 1975, Part XIVB, s 114Q.)

Reflective thinking, coercion, control, and collective compliance

This research emphasises that coercive control can be structural, existing within systems designed to regulate or support daily life, and is not just interpersonal.

This raises hard questions about where the line lies between public policy, collective safety, and individual autonomy.

Did some people view mandated COVID-19 vaccinations as coercion rather than as a necessary public health measure?

Did threatening employees with job loss or exclusion from the workplace for being unvaccinated represent institutional coercion, or was it a proportional response to protect others?

Similarly, when access to the childcare subsidy is the children's immunisation status, is this o encourage public health compliance or make up economic pressure that restricts parental choice?

Some scholars suggest that elements of systemic or policy-based coercion can mirror those same dynamics on a larger scale—particularly when fear of punishment or exclusion complies instead of informed consent, although coercive control typically dominates and entraps an individual through repeated patterns

These questions don't have simple answers, but they invite us to examine how power operates not only in intimate relationships, but within the institutions and policies that shape our everyday lives.

# When Roles Reverse: Adult Children Controlling Parents

In some families, the dynamics shift as children become adults. Parents can become vulnerable to manipulation by their own children, particularly those facing illness, ageing, or financial strain, which inverts what once appeared to be a natural hierarchy of care.

This reversal challenges common assumptions about family roles. Adult children may exploit emotional bonds, financial resources, or access to grandchildren to maintain control, leaving parents silenced by shame and bound by love. In these cases, the adult children deploy the same strategies seen in intimate partner coercive control—isolation, gaslighting, financial exploitation, and threats of abandonment—in a new direction, reshaping the family dynamic into one of fear and dependency.

## Tactics Used by Adult Children

**Financial exploitation**: demanding money, threatening estrangement if refused.

**Emotional blackmail**: "If you do not help me, you do not really care about me."

**Exploiting** grandchildren through threats against them and their relationships with them

**Isolation:** discouraging parents from contact with others to centralise control

**Blaming** a parent for a poor childhood to justify behaviour and guilt an ageing parent

Examples

A son pressures his mother to withdraw pension money, insisting, "If you loved me, you would help me."

A daughter warns her father, "Do not see those relatives; they are against you." Over time, he withdraws, leaving her as his only source of connection.

An adult child threatens, "If you do not cover my debts, you will never see your grandkids again."

You were a horrible parent to me when I was growing up. Do you remember when you did ...... You were never there for me.

## Parallels With Other Forms of Coercive Control

The tactics mirror intimate partner dynamics: isolation, guilt, conditional love, and threats of loss. What differs is the bond exploited: parental love. Parents may comply not out of agreement, but from fear of losing affection, grandchildren, or family harmony.

## Why Does It Go Unrecognised?

Shame and stigma: parents may feel humiliated admitting their child is abusive.

Family loyalty: deep bonds lead to excusing or minimising behaviour.

System blind spots: most policy and service frameworks emphasise partner violence, overlooking coercive control away from the intimate partner relationship

## Implications and Pathways Forward

Naming adult–child coercive control validates the experience of older victims and highlights the urgent need for systemic recognition. Elder abuse frameworks, financial safeguards, and professional training are responding, but awareness of coercive control dynamics in these relationships remains limited.

## Research Insight

Storey (2020) identified that many cases of elder financial abuse involve ongoing manipulation and pressure rather than one-off theft.

Quinlan, Donnelly, & O'Donnell (2024) proposed a conceptual model of filial coercive control, highlighting markers such as dependency, entrapment, intimidation, and fear—closely paralleling established frameworks of coercive control.

## How to Recognise a Healthy Friendship

Mutual respect means that both individuals value each other's needs, time, and boundaries.

Freedom: Friends encourage outside connections and celebrate independence.

Support without strings: People provide care freely, not using it as leverage or creating debt.

People can express disagreements without fearing punishment, promoting honesty and trust.

Balance: Each person can take and give without one dominating the other.

Healthy friendships foster growth and connection, not guilt or dependency.

## My journey.

After leaving an abusive relationship, I believed most of my boundary work was around intimate partners. I had learned to name coercive control, to recognise red flags, and to reclaim safety in myself. What I did not expect was how much of the same work I would need to do in my friendships.

Part of what made me vulnerable in the past was also what I valued most about myself: my kindness and instinct to care for others. Groomed at a young age to meet other people's needs, I learned to equate love with self-sacrifice. That history did not just affect how I related to partners — it also left me exposed in friendships. I often gave more than I received, overlooked red flags, and felt guilty whenever I tried to set boundaries.

The hardest realisation was this: even after all the work I had done in intimate relationships, I still had to face how I attracted friends who repeated the same controlling patterns. I would give anyone a chance and welcome anyone into my home. I did not protect myself, believing that danger existed only within intimate partnerships. Eventually, I had to widen the lens and ask why I felt drawn to friendships that left me small, drained, or silenced.

Learning to set boundaries with all the people in my life has been both confronting and liberating. I have discovered that genuine friendship does not demand loyalty through guilt or dependency. It respects space, celebrates growth, and allows both people to flourish. Healing is not only about leaving the abuser behind but also about learning to choose connections that honour who we are. I learned I am not beneath anyone — and that I may have needs.

## Self-Reflection: Coercive Control Beyond Intimate Partners

Have you ever witnessed or experienced control in a friendship, workplace, or family setting that echoes the tactics described as isolation, gaslighting, financial pressure, or silencing? How did it affect your sense of autonomy?

When thinking about systems like welfare, family courts, or workplaces, do you see patterns that mirror coercive control? How does recognising these parallels change the way you view institutions that support or protect?

How might shame or fear of judgment prevent people from speaking up when coercion comes from friends, adult children, or systems? Have you ever felt silenced in this way?

In your community or culture, are there behaviours in friendships, families, or institutions that are often dismissed as "normal" but may reflect control and coercion?

What qualities do you notice in your healthiest friendships — respect, freedom, encouragement, balance? How do these differ from the controlling dynamics described in this chapter?

# Part Two
# The Hidden Impact on Children

## Parent–Child Coercive Control

We now know that in intimate partner violence, people widely recognise coercive control as deliberate, patterned behaviour designed to dominate and entrap. The perpetrator knows what they are doing: they isolate, gaslight, monitor, and punish to secure obedience. The perpetrator intends to control, ensuring they diminish the victim's autonomy to maintain power.

With parents, the picture is more complex. Many of the same behaviours—love withdrawal, guilt, surveillance, and over control — are present, but the motives can differ:

Fear and anxiety are the roots ("If I do not control my child, something bad will happen").

Individuals learn behaviours that are repeated from their own upbringing.

It is an unconscious use of conditional regard because parents lack other tools. In these cases, the parent is not always acting with the same calculated intent as an abusive partner. Instead, they may act out of their own unresolved trauma, rigid beliefs, or cultural norms about obedience and respect.

However, intent does not erase impact. Even if a parent claims they are "protecting" or "teaching discipline," the child still experiences the dynamic as controlling, fearful, and identity-eroding.

Some parents do, in fact, consciously manipulate to maintain dominance, for example, narcissistic parents who weaponise guilt or love withdrawal to keep their children emotionally dependent.

In such cases, the parental intent aligns more closely with the deliberate coercion of perpetrators.

## Key Distinction: Power and Dependence

**In perpetrator–partner dynamics**, the control is often about maintaining dominance in a chosen relationship.

**In parent–child dynamics**, control can arise from a developmental imbalance of power that already exists.

Parents are supposed to guide, but when that guidance crosses into conditional love and manipulation, it becomes coercive.

Many behaviours overlap, but the intent may range:

**Unconsciously or misguided**, parents use conditional regard or over control without recognising the harm.

**Conscious but justified**: parents knowingly manipulating but telling themselves it is "for the child's own good."

**Deliberate domination**: parents who mirror perpetrator intent by exploiting dependency to maintain long-term control.

People often dismiss coercive control in families as "discipline" or "care." Research shows these behaviours can carry deep developmental and psychological costs. Parents may justify excessive control as protection, but it ultimately undermines autonomy. Studies show that children experiencing intrusive parenting are more likely to develop anxiety, poor self-regulation, and low self-esteem

Parents may use emotional manipulation, whether consciously or unconsciously, to secure compliance. Unlike occasional guilt-tripping, this is systematic and conditional.

Forward and Frazier (1997) describe this as manipulation with demands, threats, and exploitation of bonds.

In practice:

"If you loved me, you would not hurt me like this."

"After all I have done for you, this is how you repay me?"


Assor, Roth, and Deci (2004) explain how conditional regard—when parents withhold affection if children cannot meet expectations—can lead to emotional costs and poorer psychological outcomes.

Monitoring diaries, phones, or movements may look protective, but it undermines the developmental need for privacy. People widely recognise privacy as critical for autonomy, identity formation, and healthy peer relationships (see Petronio, 2002).

When children must meet their parents' emotional or practical needs, often at the expense of their own developmental needs, parentification happens, leading to guilt, role confusion, and later relational difficulties (Hooper, 2007).

Children raised with conditional love and coercion often internalise the belief: "I am only valuable if I please others." Research shows that this can contribute to anxious attachment in adulthood (Mikulincer & Shaver, 2007), as well as perfectionism and overcompliance, and increased vulnerability in relationships where conditional love or control feels familiar.

## Examples of Deliberate Parent–Child Coercive Control

Example 1: Guilt and Emotional Blackmail
A teenager wants to join a sports team. The parent says, "You only care about yourself. If you loved me, you would stay home to help me instead." The child silences their desires to maintain closeness.

Example 2: Isolation and Manufactured Fear
A 10-year-old wants to attend a friend's party. The parent insists: "The world is full of liars and abusers; if you go, you will get hurt." Over time, the child withdraws from peers, believing only the parent is the only form of safe. The parent intends to maintain dependency and financial benefits linked to care.

Example 3: Role Reversal and Obligation
An adolescent comforts a parent after a breakup. The parent says, "If you leave me alone, I do not know what I will do." The child misses' school to support them, learning that their value lies in meeting the parent's emotional needs.

# Role Reversal, Parentification, and Coercive Control Through Children

Parentification occurs when children must meet their parents' needs instead of their own. Instead of receiving care, the child becomes the caretaker, suppressing their needs to maintain family stability. This reversal can lead to feelings of guilt, role confusion, and relational difficulties that persist well into adulthood (Hooper, 2007; Jurkovic, 1997).

In family and domestic violence, parentification can intersect with coercive control in particularly damaging ways. A controlling parent may deliberately use the child to punish, undermine, or destabilise the other parent. This can include sabotaging the child's bond with the other caregiver, pressuring them to take sides, or interfering with communication and contact. Such behaviour co-opts the child into the dynamics of abuse, effectively turning them into an instrument of control rather than an independent developing individual.

Emma Katz (2022) has documented how children and non-abusive parents often become co-victims and co-survivors of coercive control. One distinct tactic involves the perpetrator's deliberate undermining of the child's relationship with the other parent, such as restricting contact, spreading distortions, or creating conflict during transitions. These tactics erode trust and fracture family bonds, leaving children caught in divided loyalties.

Amanda Sillars (2017, 2023) further describes how parental alienating behaviours function as coercive control, not simply as conflict. Such behaviour includes negative narratives, blame, half-truths, interrogating children about the other parent, and emotionally charged changeovers. Over time, this might cause what Sillars calls "trauma-coerced attachment" — where fear, manipulation, and pressure shape a child's loyalty, rather than genuine safety or relational choice.

When children are in this position, it compromises their development. They may internalise messages such as, "I am only valued if I comply", struggle with autonomy, and carry patterns of over-compliance or anxious attachment into adulthood. The impact is twofold: someone robs children of their right to unconditional care, and the targeted parent suffers the deep rupture of someone using their relationship as a weapon of control.

By broadening the lens beyond intimate partners, we see coercive control as a relational pattern that can emerge wherever power and dependency intersect. Naming these dynamics creates pathways for change — for parents to replace coercion with guidance and for society to recognise that control is never a substitute for connection.

# Children and Coercive Control

This chapter examines how coercive control influences a child's emotional world, attachment patterns, and brain development. Recognising these effects on children is critical for prevention, protection and recovery. Children who grow up around coercive control live inside the abuse — they do not just observe it. However, too often, systems cannot see coercive control as directly harmful to children, leaving them without adequate protection from its devastating and lasting effects.

## The Psychological Impact on Children

Children exposed to coercive control live in an environment of chronic stress. Their developing brains and bodies adapt to survive, but those who cannot see the bigger picture often misinterpret these survival strategies as problems. Instead, they often mislabel their behaviour as disobedience, laziness, or pathological, rather than understanding it as a trauma response.

Common effects include:

### Hypervigilance

Many children become experts at scanning for danger. They notice the shift in a parent's footsteps, tone of voice, or facial expression long before others do. What outsiders might dismiss as oversensitivity is, in fact, a finely tuned survival skill.

### Anxiety and Depression

Living with ongoing fear and unpredictability can

create a constant state of internal alarm. This may show up as panic attacks, nightmares, difficulty sleeping, or a persistent low mood. For some, it becomes the backdrop of their entire childhood.

## Behavioural Challenges
Survival looks different for every child. Some fight back through aggression, tantrums, or defiance. Others disappear into themselves, becoming quiet, compliant, and invisible to avoid attracting conflict. Both patterns are adaptive responses to an unsafe environment.

## Cognitive Load
Survival mode consumes enormous mental energy. When a child's developing brain is jam-packed with monitoring a threat, teachers might see poor attention, but vigilance is exhausted.

## Shame and Guilt
Perpetrators of coercive control frequently blame children for conflict or force them to take sides. Children may carry the belief that they caused the abuse or failed to protect the non-abusive parent. Over time, this instils feelings of responsibility, guilt, and shame that often persist into adulthood.

## Relationship Templates
Children often absorb distorted ideas of what relationships look like. If children normalise secrecy, fear, or dominance, these patterns can later carry over into peer friendships, intimate relationships, and even professional settings.

These effects are often invisible. A teacher may see a disruptive or clingy child without realising these are symptoms of survival. A counsellor might misdiagnose anxiety or attention disorders without asking what the home environment is like. When context is missing, children risk being punished, misunderstood, or medicated for behaviours that are essentially coping strategies in response to ongoing trauma.

## Neurological Effects

Coercive control not only shapes how children feel, but it can also alter the architecture of their developing brains. When a child lives in constant fear, their nervous system adapts by remaining in a state of high alert. Over time, this heightened stress response rewires key brain structures in ways that affect behaviour, learning, and long-term health.

Key effects include:

### Amygdala
The brain's alarm centre becomes overactive, primed to detect the smallest signals of threat. This leaves children easily startled and quick to react as though danger is ever-present.

### Prefrontal Cortex
Chronic stress can slow the development of the brain's "thinking" region, which governs impulse control, decision-making, and emotional regulation. As a result, children may struggle to calm down, manage their frustration, or plan effectively.

### Hippocampus
Prolonged exposure to heightened levels of cortisol (the body's stress hormone), can cause the memory

and learning centre to shrink. Children may struggle to recall instructions, absorb new information, or maintain focus in school.

## Testing Neurological Effects

Research shows that coercive control can alter brain development. However, specialised imaging, such as MRI, detects most structural changes in areas like the amygdala, prefrontal cortex, and hippocampus.

Professionals can assess the functional effects: difficulties with attention, memory, sleep, or emotional regulation. Professionals usually measure these through neuropsychological assessments, behavioural observations, and questionnaires, which clarify how trauma appears in daily life.

## Cortisol

Cortisol, often referred to as the primary stress hormone, is a key biological marker of stress. Researchers can measure it in blood, saliva, urine, and hair samples.

Blood or saliva tests provide an immediate or snapshot level of cortisol, showing how the hypothalamic-pituitary-adrenal (HPA) axis is functioning in the short term.

Hair cortisol testing is a relatively new method used primarily in research. It provides a retrospective view by integrating cortisol exposure over weeks to months.

Elevated or dysregulated cortisol levels are often associated with chronic stress, trauma, or dysregulation of the HPA axis. Many studies link these associations to children exposed to adversity and ongoing stress, such as that seen in coercive control.When we use the phrase stress being in the body, we typically measure cortisol as the hormone.

## Pyrroles

Practitioners can also assess for elevated levels of pyrroles, as these may contribute to adverse mental health symptoms such as mood swings, poor stress tolerance, or anxiety. The medical community widely rejects this testing because of its controversy.

## My journey

I took my child to the Sydney Developmental Clinic after fruitlessly trying to access support. They struggled with restlessness, difficulty focusing, and emotional outbursts, which were too often dismissed as inappropriate behaviour.

As part of that appointment, my child had a brain map (EEG) taken. The technician gently placed electrodes on the scalp and then recorded quietly for a brief session. The technician later showed me a colourful brain map, which highlighted areas of over- or under-activity.

For me, this data was powerful. It was not just another opinion; it was tangible evidence that helped explain what my child was experiencing. It did not replace the careful work of history-taking and clinical assessment, but it added another layer of confidence to the diagnosis and treatment plan. What made the actual difference was having professionals who could interpret the EGG within the broader context of my child's life.

## The Risk of Misinterpretation

Research has shown that trauma symptoms are frequently mistaken for neurodevelopmental disorders. Ford et al. (2013) noted that children exposed to complex trauma often meet diagnostic criteria for multiple disorders, even though the root cause is unresolved trauma. Researcher Van der Kolk (2014) similarly warns that without understanding trauma, professionals risk treating the symptoms while missing the underlying survival adaptations.

Because these effects are invisible, people sometimes misdiagnose children with ADHD, Oppositional Defiant Disorder (ODD), or label them as lazy or difficult when their brains are working hard to ensure their survival. People could mistake hypervigilance for inattention, misinterpret emotional outbursts as defiance, and misinterpret withdrawal as disinterest. People easily neglect these trauma-driven behaviours without recognising coercive control.

This misinterpretation carries genuine risks. Interventions such as medication or rigid behavioural programs, when applied without a trauma-informed lens, can deepen shame. This may reinforce the child's sense of failure and leave them feeling even more unsafe. Instead of relief, the child can experience another layer of misunderstanding and invalidation.

Training for teachers, doctors, psychologists, and child-protection workers is therefore crucial. When professionals understand the bigger picture, they can recognise trauma and offer children what they need most: safety, which is the strongest foundation for healing.

A misdiagnosis can expose a child to medication treatment that may not be required.

## Physical Effects of Coercive Control on Children

Coercive control does not just shape children's emotions and behaviour — it also shows up in their bodies. Chronic stress from living in an unsafe environment can disrupt basic biological systems and leave lasting marks on physical health.

Common physical effects include:

Sleep disturbances: nightmares, broken sleep, or complete insomnia caused by a body that never feels safe enough to rest.

Frequent stomach aches or headaches, often triggered by stress hormones flooding the system.

Prolonged activation of the stress response can lead to weakened immune systems and slower recovery from everyday illnesses.

Survival diverts energy away from growth, leading to growth and developmental delays.

Somatic pain with no apparent medical cause, such as muscle aches, chest pains, or dizziness.

Eating difficulties may stem from stress, hypervigilance during meals, or the perpetrator's control over food.

## How can it present?

Child 1
A seven-year-old child was experiencing daily stomach aches and frequent nightmares while living in a household marked by coercive control. Medical

investigations found no underlying illness. After the parents separated and the child moved into a calmer, more predictable environment, the symptoms rapidly improved. Within two months, the stomach-aches stopped, and sleep became restful. This shows that children's bodies often signal distress before they can explain it, and how quickly health can recover when the stressor is gone.

Child 2:

A doctor diagnosed a 12-year-old child with a functional neurological disorder after the child experienced an unexplained loss of movement in the limbs. Extensive medical testing could not identify an organic cause. Investigators subsequently discovered the child lived in a high-conflict home marked by extreme coercive control. The child's body had found its own way of expressing overwhelming stress through physical symptoms. When the child felt safe and stable, the episodes became less frequent and severe, illustrating the close connection between the child's nervous system and their surroundings.

**Children as Mirrors**

When children grow up inside coercive control, they sometimes reflect the very behaviours they have witnessed. Survivors describe moments when their own children use the abuser's tone, repeat their language, or even direct violence at them. Having a child you love harm you is one of the most painful parts of anyone experiencing this journey. While you know they are also victims of their forced environment.

Children mirror for different reasons.

**Learned patterns**: They have seen that power and control work and copied it to feel strong.

**Loyalty binds**: to survive, they may align with the perpetrator, turning their anger onto the safer parent.

**Unprocessed trauma**: hypervigilance, fear, and confusion can explode outward as aggression.

This behaviour does not mean children are bad or beyond repair. It is a symptom of the violence they have endured. They are acting out what they have normalised, often without understanding the harm it causes.

For the survivor parent, this can feel like a double betrayal: first being hurt by the abuser and then being broken again through the child who has absorbed their tactics. Shame and grief often follow the question, what did I do wrong? How did I let this happen? Parents entrapped in coercive control themselves cannot fully protect their children from it.

Support of these families must hold both truths: Children who mirror abusive behaviour are victims, not villains.

Survivor parents deserve compassion and practical help, not judgment, when facing violence from their children.


I think it is important for me to share that this issue is very real, and we are observing an increase in restraint orders within the parent-child relationship because of domestic violence and coercive control.

I have engaged in many confidential discussions with individuals who feel unable to disclose their identities because of the shame associated with experiencing abuse from their children. Many parents face a difficult balance between ensuring their own safety and maintaining their love and loyalty for their children.

Naming this openly helps break the silence. It reminds parents they are not alone and reminds society that the impact of coercive control does not end with the partner relationship. Without caring and understanding intervention, future generations will also experience a repeat of the pattern.

**"It was not just my partner shouting or controlling me anymore. It was my child, using the exact words, with the same look. I cannot describe how broken I was."**
**— Survivor.**

### Indoctrination and Shaping Reality

Coercive control does more than create emotional wounds and physical symptoms — it reshapes a child's entire sense of reality. Perpetrators might indoctrinate children to believe that one caregiver is dangerous, that they cannot trust extended family, or that love must always be conditional. Over time, these messages distort how they relate not only to parents, but to friends, teachers, and peers.

Instead of approaching relationships with openness, children may become guarded, suspicious, or overly loyal to one side. Trust feels unsafe, affection feels like a test, and belonging feels fragile. This distorted lens can leave children isolated, cut off from the very support networks that could help them heal. The impact of coercive control can follow children into adolescence and adulthood. It can shape how they connect, who they trust, and what they believe they deserve in relationships. A perpetrator inflicts this on a child to have control, and this rewrites long-term generational narratives and causes identities to be lost.

## Fractured relationship

One child, who once ran joyfully to greet a parent at every visit, gradually pulled away. At first, it was small: less eye contact, shorter hugs, a nervous glance toward the other caregiver. Over time, the warmth disappeared altogether.

The child began repeating phrases that sounded rehearsed: 'You do not really care about me,' 'You only want me to win in court' Then, someone planted and repeated false allegations.

Something fractured a secure and loving bond. Isolation and indoctrination taught the child to fear and reject the parent who had once been their safe base. This process left the child cut off from love and caught in a confusing web of loyalty they could not escape.

"When children echo coercive control, they are not the problem; they are the proof of the problem."

# A Parallel Story: Cult Indoctrination

## The Peoples Temple

In the 1950s, preacher Jim Jones began the People's Temple as a movement for equality and social justice. Members initially described how they felt inspired by a diverse community that welcomed them and promised fairness, care, and a sense of belonging.

However, over time, minor signs of control emerged. Control tightened. Members were told who they could spend time with and instructed to sever connections with friends and family outside of the group. When individuals doubted Jim Jones, the leader, those doubts were reframed as betrayal. They asked members to repeat loyalty phrases and denounce "outsiders" as dangerous. Eventually, many accepted distorted realities, even when those contradicted their own memories and instincts.

This gradual reshaping of thought, language, and loyalty is the essence of indoctrination. It can draw intelligent, caring people into silencing their true selves.

## Heaven's Gate:

Heaven's Gate was a US religious movement founded in the 1970s by Marshall Applewhite and Bonnie Nettles. It combined elements of Christianity, New Age spirituality, and UFO beliefs. The central teaching: Earth was about to be "recycled" and salvation meant leaving behind one's human identity to join a higher, extraterrestrial existence.

Leaders controlled and persuaded members to sever ties with family and friends, which reinforced their total reliance on the group.

They gave up their possessions, money, and often their names — adopting new identities that aligned with the group's doctrine.

Strictly regulating clothing, diet, and behaviour reinforced uniformity and obedience in daily life.

They framed doubts as spiritual weakness or a failure of commitment.

Leaders used repetition of doctrine, communal living, and isolation from outsiders to strengthen group loyalty.

Members were told that their survival and eternal purpose depended on obedience.

Some even underwent voluntary castration to suppress sexual desire, framed as a step toward higher existence — showing the extent of influence.

A tragedy happened in March 1997, a comet passed close to Earth, and Applewhite told followers that a spacecraft hidden behind the comet would take them to salvation.

Over thirty-nine members died by mass suicide, believing death was their passage to the next level.

## Why This Matters for Understanding Coercive Control?

Heaven's Gate shows the hallmarks of coercive control and indoctrination:

**Isolation:** Members experience being cut off from family and friends, mirroring how children in coercively controlled families may experience isolation from one parent.

**Surveillance & Uniformity**: Strict rules over dress, food, and behaviour mirror micro-regulation in coercive relationships.

**Repetition of doctrine**: Constant teaching replaced members' independent thinking with the leader's narrative — just as children may repeat rehearsed phrases about a parent.

**Fear of abandonment**: Members believed leaving the group meant losing salvation; children in coercive dynamics fear losing love or safety if they resist.

Indoctrination does not require physical violence — it works by slowly reshaping reality, isolating people from alternative perspectives, and binding them through fear, guilt, and conditional belonging.

The same dynamics can occur in families where a child, out of fear or loyalty, learns to echo the narratives of a controlling parent, even against their own lived experience

of love and safety.

The People's Temple and Heaven's Gate examples show how adults can become victims, falling into systems of indoctrination that are so strong they break identity, loyalty, and family bonds. In the aftermath of such tragedies, society often recognises the harm and calls for investigation, reform, or intervention. However, when children experience parallel processes of coercive control inside their own families, the response is far less consistent.

Children may echo rehearsed phrases, withdraw from once-trusted parents, or display signs of fear and divided loyalty. However, people too often minimise these behaviours as "conflict" or dismiss them as a child's choice without understanding the actual circumstances.

# Through Children's Eyes: Life Inside Coercive Control

Children who grow up subjected to coercive control live with fear, confusion, and divided loyalties woven into their everyday lives. These examples, drawn from children's actual experiences, illustrate how coercive control affects everyday routines, including school, meals, family contact, and bedtime.

This is not a matter of isolated incidents or misunderstandings. They are deliberate patterns that keep children anxious, conflicted, and hyperaware of adult moods. By stepping into these days of life, we can see coercive control not as an abstract concept, but as a lived reality that shapes every aspect of childhood.

## How Children Experience Coercive Control

Children may hear or experience:

'Tell them they are pathetic.' 'Ask them why they are such terrible parent.'

The interrogators questioned them about the other household, including their destinations, acquaintances, and spending habits.

Hearing constant criticism: 'It is their fault you are late for school,' 'they are useless with money,' 'if it were not for them, we would be happy.'

One caregiver indoctrinates and coerces a child to feel responsible for their happiness.

A child receives emotional punishment if they show affection for someone else.

A child may receive gifts or money as a reward for ignoring the other parent.

Someone gives the child a pet, and when the child wants to visit the other caregiver, people pressure the child into believing their pet will be sad without them or that they feed the pet every day, which encourages isolation.

Conflicting rules: a child is confused; one home says yes, the other says no.

A child who has their phone calls withheld, or calls put on a speaker, and video chats can make the child feel cut off, isolated and under surveillance.

Secrets or false information that undermine trust and turn the child against the other caregiver.

One parent manipulates the communication intended for the child.

A child must take sides in front of siblings, relatives, or even professionals.

The theme:
These are not neutral or accidental events. They are deliberate strategies of coercive control.

## Child 1: Indoctrination Through Fear

A ten-year-old child throws away packed lunches and refuses to eat. When asked why, the child explains: 'They told me you were trying to poison me.'
The child does not hate the other caregiver; they are frightened and confused. These planted messages make the child feel unsafe in both homes. Over time,

stomach aches emerge on contact days, and both sleep and schoolwork suffer.

## Child 2: Isolation from Extended Family

An eight-year-old child refuses phone calls from extended family. When relatives try to connect, the child responds:
'I am not allowed to talk to you anymore. You are dangerous.'
The controlling caregiver has rehearsed and repeated these words almost verbatim. Soon, the child withdraws completely from grandparents, cousins, and family friends. What appears to be rejection is indoctrination — a strategy designed to cut the child off from their entire support network.

## Child 3: Loyalty Testing and Conflicted Love

A twelve-year-old child is told again and again that the other parent "does not love you" and "only cares about money." At first, the child resists, insisting that both parents love them. Over time, the constant repetition wears them down. The child grows fearful of visits, convinced they are unwelcome. At school, the child confides in a teacher.
"If I choose one parent, I lose the other. I do not know who I am allowed to love." This confusion leaves the child anxious, withdrawn, and mistrustful of relationships.

## Child 4: Punishment for Joy and Connection

A nine-year-old child came home from a visit with extended family, excited about a birthday celebration. The controlling caregiver responded with icy silence

and then snapped:
'So you would rather be with them than with me.'

The child quickly learned that showing joy about time with relatives meant punishment through rejection, guilt, or anger. Soon, the child stopped talking about family altogether, erasing those experiences to stay safe.

### Child 5: Daily Loyalty Tests

A child wakes up rehearsing what not to say, fearing that a single wrong word might upset a parent. Breakfast is quiet, because one slip could spark anger. At school, the class is making gifts for parents to celebrate Easter. The child wants to create something for both parents but knows this is impossible. To avoid choosing, the child misbehaved, and the teacher sent them out of the classroom. Guilt weighs heavily — they cannot make gifts for both, and now they have disappointed their teacher as well. After school, the questioning begins: "What did you do today?" The child knows that the "wrong" answer could lead to tears, accusations, or hours of silence. Before sleep, the child wonders: "Am I bad for missing them? Am I betraying someone?" The loyalty test never ends, leaving the child trapped in a cycle of fear and guilt.

### Child 6: Digital Surveillance and Message Control

Before breakfast, the child is told, 'Do not open any messages from the other parent — they are only trying to cause trouble.' A knot forms in the child's stomach, but they nod silently. At school, a teacher mentions sending out an email about an upcoming excursion.

The child panics, unsure of what is "allowed" to be said, and quickly changes the subject. After school, the child needs to return the phone immediately. They interrogate about any missed calls: 'Who tried to reach you? 'What did they want?' When making a call to a friend, the caregiver puts it on speakerphone and listens in, sometimes ending the call mid-conversation. The child deletes harmless messages by evening because they are afraid of being accused of "keeping secrets." In bed, the child nervously scrolls through notifications one last time, fearing someone will misinterpret something innocent as evidence of disloyalty. Even sleep offers a brief escape; the feeling of being constantly watched follows into dreams.

## Child 7: Isolation Through School Sabotage

Morning
A child is told they do not have to go to school because 'the teachers are on the other parent's side.' What starts as an occasional absence becomes a frequent one.

School Day
Friends ask why the child is not at school; rumours start. The child feels isolated from their peers and loses confidence in their learning.

After School
The controlling caregiver rewards the child for staying home with treats, games, or special outings, reinforcing the belief that school (and the other parent) is unsafe.

The child lies in bed in the evening, believing that education is dangerous and distrusting the world outside the home.

## Child 8: Weaponising Siblings

Morning
Two siblings get ready for school. Someone praises one: 'You are the good one. "Why can't you be more like them? Alternatively, you are just like your other parent." These remarks are not casual.

School Day
At school, the siblings sit apart at lunch. Resentment and rivalry simmer because one feels favoured while the other feels rejected. Instead of building a secure sibling bond, coercive control twists natural differences in fuel for mistrust.

After School
When they return home, one sibling receives a treat for showing loyalty. Therefore, they ignore the other sibling. They make it clear: children must earn affection by complying, and parents punish by withholding love.

Evening
Arguments break out between the siblings. They deliberately turned a potential source of support into a source of competition. Coercive control fractures the sibling relationship, leaving the children isolated from each other instead of united.

## Child 9: Confusion About Love and Safety

Morning
A child wakes up to a surprise gift and is told, 'I love you more than anyone' However, the child's joy quickly turns to fear when the caregiver withdraws affection later that day for mentioning the other parent.

School Day
In class, the child struggles to focus, replaying the confusing shift from love to rejection. Classmates talk about hugs and bedtime stories; the child feels unsure what love even means.

After School
The child is told, 'If you really loved me, you would not want to go there.' Love becomes conditional, tied to rejecting the other caregiver.

Evening
The child goes to bed holding the gift but feeling sick with anxiety, unsure if tomorrow will bring affection or punishment.

## Child 10: Silencing and Secrets

In the morning, someone warns the child, "If you tell anyone what is happening here, they will take you away — and it will be your fault." The message clearly demands silence and places the burden of protection on the child.

At school, when a teacher notices sadness and gently asks what is wrong, the child forces a smile. Fear of "causing trouble" keeps them from speaking. Coercive control ensures that even safe adults feel unsafe to trust.

After school, the child overhears adult conversations about money, court, or threats. They are told: "What happens here stays between us," or "Your other parent is just making trouble... they do not even care about you." Adults turn the child into a keeper of their secrets, trapping them between loyalty, fear, and confusion.

Lying in bed, the child silently rehearses the secrets, terrified of making a mistake. The weight of adult responsibilities presses down, stealing their freedom to be a child simply. Coercive control turns childhood into a careful performance of silence.

## Child 11: Identity and Belonging

The day starts; the child is told while getting dressed, "Do not wear that — you look just like them." The child chooses clothes, not for comfort, but to avoid looking like the other caregiver.

At school, the child hides drawings or interests that resemble the other side of the family, fearing criticism if discovered.

After school, the caregiver pressures the child to take on hobbies or roles that mirror their identity, saying, 'This is who we are.' 'If you love me, you will be loyal to me... not like the parent. They were not loyal to the family and left you.'

At night alone, the child wonders, 'Am I allowed to be myself?' Or do I have to be who they want me to be?" Did my other parent leave me?"

## Child 12: Loss of Childhood Freedoms

In the morning, the child wanted to play at a friend's house but got denied because someone said, "Friends are not trustworthy."

During the school day, the child feels left out and ashamed because they cannot explain why someone prevents them from joining in.

At night, the child lies in bed longing for ordinary

freedom, sleepovers, playdates, or carefree laughter, all things stolen by coercive control.

## Child 12 - System Manipulation

Before the family court appointment in the morning, someone indoctrinates the child: "Remember what to say. "If you make a mistake, they will take you away, and you will never see me again." "The other parent does not love you; they only want to take you away from me. "

In class, the child zones out, practising the script instead of listening to the teacher. Anxiety builds about making a mistake.

After school, the child, in fear and loyalty, rehearsed lines to professionals: 'I do not want to see them. They scare me.' The words are not entirely theirs but feel impossible to resist. The seeds planted by the other parent, not loving them, sat in the back of their minds.

Alone in bed, the child whispers the truth to a stuffed toy: 'I miss them, but I cannot say it.'

Children rarely have the words to describe what is happening around them, but their behaviour becomes their language. When coercive control isolates a child from a once-loving parent, their outward behaviour can reflect the confusion and loyalty conflicts they feel inside.

After a period of isolation or exposure to one parent's controlling narrative, a child may show:

**Sudden rejection or fear** toward the previously loved parent, insisting they don't want contact or claiming that parent is "bad" or "unsafe."

**Contradictory emotions**, such as distress when the parent leaves but hostility when they arrive.

**Behavioural difficulties** — anger, aggression, withdrawal, or emotional outbursts — that seem out of character or appear mainly around transitions or discussions of the other parent.

**Language and phrases** that sound adult or rehearsed, mirroring the controlling parent's words or tone.

**Hyper-vigilance or people-pleasing**, trying to anticipate what will keep the controlling parent calm.

**Regression or anxiety symptoms**, such as sleep problems, stomach aches, or difficulty concentrating at school.

These behaviours are not evidence of a child's genuine dislike or fear of the other parent, but often a sign of loyalty conflict, trauma bonding, and emotional survival.

**"When children live within coercive control, their behaviour tells the story their words cannot form."**

### Research Insight

I once had a child protection worker advise that a child often rejects their protective parent, as they know it is safe to do so, and the love is unconditional. As much as I tried to find a source, I could not. What I could locate was not definite; however, consistent research findings suggest that in coercive control dynamics, children may distance themselves even from the more protective parent, as if rejecting safety under pressure. Loyalty shifting can become an act of survival rather than a matter of preference.

# Who Protects the Children? When Child Protection and Family Law Collide.

In my professional career and lived experience, I have observed a consistent pattern: child protection agencies frequently hand off cases to the family court. One worker even told me, "Child protection authorities do not intervene in family law matters.

That left me thinking, is not coercive control emotional and psychological abuse? Isn't that child abuse? Survivors are stuck in this confusion, attempting to alert others about their children while two systems argue about who should act.

I have an email from a Chief Justice of the Family Court advising that they cannot intervene in state child protection matters.

## What the Law Says

Under the Family Law Act 1975 (Cth), courts must consider family violence when making parenting orders. Courts also recognise children's exposure to this behaviour as family violence.

State law: In every Australian jurisdiction, child protection legislation defines harm or risk of significant harm to include psychological harm or exposure to family violence. Therefore, state child protection agencies can and should intervene when children experience coercive control.

## Where the Gaps and Conflicts Happen

Despite these laws, practice tells another story:

Screening out cases: Agencies often reject reports of emotional abuse if there is no physical injury or immediate threat. Risk assessments remain geared towards visible harm.

Hand balling to family law: Agencies such as Child Protection Authorities may refuse to intervene once family court proceedings begin, even though state child protection powers continue to apply.

Family law's burden of proof: The Federal Circuit and Family Court of Australia must consider family violence, but proving psychological abuse requires lengthy reports, expert testimony, and cross-examination. Survivors face steep barriers, while perpetrators exploit the lack of visible proof.

Children experiencing coercive control might systematically isolate themselves from the safe caregiver, and others may indoctrinate them to fear, resent, or reject that caregiver. Agencies and courts sometimes misinterpret these manipulated beliefs as the child's authentic views, dismissing the protective parent and reinforcing unsafe arrangements.

**Psychological Abuse Overlooked**

**Invisible harm**: Emotional abuse leaves no physical bruises. Schools, therapists, or long-term patterns may provide evidence, but people easily minimise this evidence.

**High thresholds**: Systems often require proof of "significant damage" to a child's development before acting. They set the bar unrealistically high.

**Slow recognition of coercive control**: Legal definitions are developing, but frontline practice lags. Training gaps mean children living with coercive control continue to fall through the cracks.

**Misunderstanding of child behaviour and trauma**: Children exposed to coercive control often show distress through anxiety, anger, withdrawal, or rejecting the protective parent. Professionals frequently misinterpret these trauma responses as behavioural problems, disobedience, or evidence of parental alienation, instead of signs of psychological harm. Without a trauma-informed lens, children's cries for help are overlooked or even turned against the safe caregiver.

### Lack of knowledge about children, coercive control, and indoctrination.

While coercive control is slowly gaining recognition in relation to intimate partner violence, there is far less awareness of how it affects children. Many professionals lack knowledge of how to assess the impact of coercive control on a child. For example, being indoctrinated by a potentially unsafe parent, isolated from friends, or forced into loyalty conflicts can highlight these instances. People without this knowledge minimise or misunderstand children's experiences, delaying protective action.

### Case Study & Jurisdictional Comparison

A 9-year-old lives in a home where one parent constantly monitors their movements, dictates what they wear, and isolates them from friends. The child is told daily: "If you do not do what I say, your other parent will leave you."

Over time, the child develops anxiety, bed-wetting, nightmares, and a fear of speaking freely. They also parrot the controlling parent's words, repeating accusations against the safe caregiver and rejecting contact — not because of genuine preference, but because of sustained indoctrination and isolation.

## Responses Across Australia

New South Wales may meet the "Risk of Significant Harm" threshold and refer the case to the Child Protection Helpline.

Victoria requires proof of both "significant damage" and parental failure to protect. When the safe parent is active, authorities often divert cases to community services.

In Queensland, the authorities often handle emotional harm as a family-support issue rather than statutory intervention, even though it meets the statutory definition of "harm" without physical risk.

SA, WA, TAS, ACT, NT: They legally recognise emotional harm, but they often screen out cases as "family law matters" when they identify a protective parent.

## The Pattern

On paper, every jurisdiction recognises emotional and psychological harm as child abuse. The responses are inconsistent and often depend on whether others perceive a parent as protective enough. This narrow view ignores the reality that coercive control can warp a child's beliefs and behaviour, leaving them rejecting the safe caregiver while aligning with the abusive one.

This creates dangerous gaps whereby affected children remain unprotected, their voices manipulated or unheard, and their trauma minimised. The latter can include serious conflicts of loyalty.

## Family Court Limitations and the Need for Reform

Despite the 2024 amendments to the Family Law Act, which removed the presumption of equal shared parental responsibility and required courts to prioritise child safety, many families report minor changes in practice.

Key Challenges

**Coercive control and distorted beliefs**: children may reject or fear the safe caregiver because of manipulation. Courts sometimes misinterpret this as the child's authentic wishes.

**Evidentiary barriers:** Without physical proof, people dismiss pattern-based abuse as allegations

 **Length of proceedings**: Proceedings can take 12–24 months, leaving children in unsafe contact

**Delays in Testing Allegations**: Allegations can take 12–24 months (or longer) to resolve through reports, cross-examination, and hearings. During this time, children are often required to maintain contact with the abusive parent, entrenching fear and trauma. Alternatively, the child has no contact with the protective parent. Allowing distorted beliefs to take hold.

**Family report writers and single experts** do not always understand the training, coercive control, or trauma-informed practice. There appears to be a lack of understanding in indoctrination education, and upon further examination, the question of why becomes more apparent.

**Family report writer assessments** may be as brief as one to two hours, missing critical patterns of psychological abuse. These reports carry enormous weight in judicial decision-making.

**Independent Children's Lawyers** receive training as lawyers, not as experts in child behaviour, trauma, coercive control, or indoctrination. This means they may lack the skills to interpret a child's expressions of fear or distress through a developmental and psychological lens. Too often, people reframe children's genuine trauma responses as resistance, parental influence, or "alignment" with one parent. This raises a larger question: if the child's best interests are served, should only lawyers fulfil this role?

**Implementation gaps:** Despite reforms, practice varies across registries. Initiatives like the Lighthouse Project are promising, but not yet fully embedded. Once the understanding from the Lighthouse Project ends, the following process lacks the same level of understanding, education, and awareness.

## Why Reform Is Urgent: The Protection Gap for Children

Adults can seek immediate protection through police-issued AVOs or exclusion orders. Children, however, must rely on slower child-protection assessments and family-law litigation. During these delays, abusive parents manipulate children's views, sabotage relationships with the safe caregiver, and deepen loyalty conflicts, which courts may then mistake for the child's authentic voice.

The problem does not rest solely with family law. Child protection systems also require urgent reform. Agencies too often screen out reports of coercive control, treat emotional abuse as a "family law matter," or cannot recognise indoctrination and isolation in affected children. These systems need urgent reform before they inflict further harm on children.

## The Call for Transparency and Accountability

Remove the hidden walls in the Family Law Court for transparency and accountability. Establish independent oversight where harm occurs despite court involvement.

Establish prominent roles and responsibilities of who is to respond to domestic violence and coercive control matters. These cases are not family law matters; they are child abuse and require child safety interventions.

Accountability is not about blame. It is about ensuring children's right to safety and preventing repeated failures.

## Intersectionality & Vulnerability

Coercive control does not affect all families equally. Overlapping factors, including disability, poverty, migration status, culture, and sexuality, shape its impact. These intersections can amplify vulnerability while also creating new safety barriers.

Disability: Systems often overlook how reliance on a caregiver can become a tool for coercive control. Survivors with disabilities may face additional coercion through restricted access to mobility aids, medication, or support services. Children with disabilities can be doubly vulnerable because someone might use their needs to entrench dependency.

Poverty: Financial dependence intensifies coercive dynamics, trapping survivors through lack of housing, transport, or income support. For children, poverty compounds trauma: limited access to counselling, disrupted schooling, and ongoing housing instability all weaken protective factors.

Abusers could threaten migrants and refugees with visa cancellation, deportation, or community isolation, language barriers and fear of the authorities' silence on disclosures.

In family law, this can cause protective parents to have less ability to present evidence, while children endure prolonged, unsafe contact because of systemic inaction.

Indigenous families: Colonisation and intergenerational trauma intersect with coercive control. People may dismiss or punish disclosures rather than support them because of systemic racism and distrust of statutory services. For Indigenous children, this perpetuates cycles of removal and loss of cultural identity, deepening harm.

LGBTQ+ families: Coercive control may exploit stigma outing, or lack of service recognition. Someone may tell the survivors their experience "does not count" as domestic violence, leaving them with fewer safe pathways to help. Children in LGBTQ+ families may also face service providers who cannot understand or respect their family structures, further silencing their voices.

These layers show why a one-size-fits-all response is insufficient. For services and courts to recognise coercive control in all its forms and respond with cultural safety, accessibility, and inclusivity, they must equip themselves.

### From the therapy room

Only one parent came to therapy. The other had stopped all contact, and the child — once deeply bonded to both — no longer wanted to see the parent who had not carried them. What had begun as a shared dream of family had become a battleground of loyalty, fear, and control.

For ten years, both parents in a same-sex relationship nurtured, guided, and loved this child, who came into being through a donor arrangement, as their own. Biology had never been the foundation of love — only intention and care. However, after separation, the shared story fractured. The biological parent withdrew access, speaking subtly but consistently in ways that reshaped the child's perception of the other. When the matter entered the family law system, the complexity deepened. The case sat at the intersection of parental rights, genetics, and identity, revealing how the law still struggles to protect relationships that fall outside traditional frameworks. Even though both parents loved and cared for the child, legal processes often favoured biology over emotional continuity for the non-biological parent. What should have been a question of the child's well-being became entangled in procedural delay, systemic bias, and the lingering social discomfort around non-traditional families.

By the time the case reached court, the child's view had shifted completely. Once warm, they now expressed rejection and hostility. They repeated adult phrases that sounded rehearsed, carrying the weight of someone else's anger. What the court called "the child's wishes" reflected an environment that had coerced emotional allegiance.

# When the System Misreads: Case Stories of Coercive Control and Misinterpretation

This chapter shares case stories that reveal how misinterpretation by child protection authorities, family report writers, independent children's lawyers, and law courts can entrench coercive control instead of disrupting it. These stories are not unique.

Children living with coercive control often become the unseen casualties of both child protection systems and family law proceedings. People do not always understand survival behavioural strategies like fear, anger, withdrawal, or rejection of safe caregivers.

When this happens, the very systems designed to protect children can compound harm. People author reports, lawyers speak, and yet children are being misrepresented and failing through gaps with devastating consequences. Protective parents often find themselves silenced or blamed, told their efforts to safeguard their children amount to hostility, manipulation, or non-cooperation.

**When courts misinterpret a child's resistance to contact as alienation rather than protection, they risk compounding the trauma and silencing the child's voice." — Amanda Sillars, founder of the Eeny Meeny Miney Mo Foundation.**

Case Example A: The Silent Child

A 10-year-old had lived with one caregiver who regularly criticised the other. Whenever the child expressed affection for the absent caregiver, they would often feel guilty or disapproved of.

During a family report interview, the child stayed quiet. The child's silence was not a fear of honesty, but a state of

neutrality. The report writer, who recommended shared time, noted no unmistakable evidence of alienation.

Nightmares and physical symptoms emerged, worsening the child's anxiety. By the time they raised concerns again, something had already damaged the child's sense of safety and trust.


Case Example B: The Weight of Guilt

An 8-year-old was repeatedly told that spending time with one caregiver meant betraying the other. Someone pressured the child to deliver hostile messages, withdrawing affection if the child showed closeness to the absent caregiver.

When interviewed, the child expressed reluctance to see the other caregiver. The family report and ICL interpreted this as a child preference rather than the product of manipulation.


Case Example C: The Missed Pattern

Over several years, one caregiver limited the child's friendships, controlled communication, and created a narrative that the other caregiver was unsafe or uncaring.

During the proceedings, the family report acknowledged conflict but downplayed coercion because of post-separation tension. The ICL relied heavily on this report, recommending equal time.

The child's distrust grew, emotional health deteriorated, and the authorities dismissed the protective caregiver's concerns. Over 18 months passed before the authorities revisited the orders, and by that point, the harm had already become entrenched.

Case Example D: From Bonded to Broken

A child had a secure, loving relationship with one caregiver. For over 15 years, the other caregiver documented incidents of family violence. Despite this history, the abusive caregiver gradually withheld the child, cutting off contact and isolating the child from the protective parent.

By the time the matter reached family law proceedings, the now deeply isolated child repeated allegations against the protective parent. The parent, who had a history of coercion and family violence, told the report writer that they supported a relationship with the child. However, the false allegations mirrored the narrative of the abusive caregiver and did not reflect the child's prior relationship, nor the documented history of violence. The family report failed to analyse long-term manipulation critically.

The court's removal of the protective parent caused the child to lose their lifelong security base. The court didn't see how coercive control can distort a child's perception and loyalty, taking the child's apparent voice at face value.

Sometimes, the court must consider parents who will say anything to win, confident in their manipulation tactics.

## Case Example E: When Child Protection Misreads Coercive Control

For many years, ongoing controlling behaviour affected a child. These included manipulation by caregivers, control over whom the child communicated with, restriction of visits, and regular verbal threats. The protective parent had documented evidence (police reports, texts, witness statements) showing family violence over an extended period.

When someone reported to the child protection agency (e.g. state department), the response focused on whether there was physical injury or neglect. Secondary concerns were emotional reports, psychological distress, and coercive control evidence. The agency closed the case, recommending counselling and support services for the protective parent, but it took no further action. The agency's decision noted that since there was no visible injury and the child was functioning at school, it did not meet the threshold for significant harm.

Over time, the controlling parent escalated isolation; the child's anxiety increased, their school attendance declined, and they began refusing contact with the protective parent.

Because child protection had closed the case, there was no statutory supervision or oversight. Later, when family law proceedings began, the expert report relied in part on that

Earlier closure, treating emotional harm as unproven. This contributed to decisions that advantaged the controlling parent, reinforcing the coercive dynamic.

### Case Example F: Pickford & Pickford [2024] FedCFamC1A 249

Two caregivers were in a relationship for around ten years and had two children, born in 2015 and 2017. The relationship ended in 2018, and court proceedings began the following year.

Over several years, the court issued multiple interim parenting orders. The children were to spend four nights per fortnight with one caregiver and additional time during school holidays.

### Allegations and Trial Findings

One caregiver alleged a long pattern of coercive and controlling behaviour by the other. This included isolation from family and friends, monitoring of finances, and other forms of surveillance and restriction. The conflict extended to issues such as school fees, property settlement, and communication.

Initially, the trial judge accepted that the conduct, taken together, constituted a part of a pattern of coercive control. The judge declined to increase time with the parent found to have engaged in that behaviour, maintaining the existing care arrangements to preserve the children's stability.

### Appeal to the Full Court

The Full Court of the Federal Circuit and Family Court of Australia (Division 1) — the appellate division of the family law system (not the High Court) — heard the appeal of the decision. The Full Court overturned aspects of the trial decision, finding that while some behaviour was controlling, the evidence did not support all the broad findings of coercive control made at trial

The appellate court emphasised that parental conflict does not always constitute family violence. Judges must distinguish between ordinary post-separation disputes and patterns of coercive power. The court sent the matter back for further consideration, thus prolonging litigation and uncertainty for the children and causing the protective caregiver to face renewed proceedings.

This case highlights how the developing recognition of coercive control intersects with the evidentiary and procedural complexities of family law. It also emphasises the risk that survivors could experience repeated conflict if appeals narrow or overturn judicial decisions about coercive dynamics.

## Patterns Emerging from the Cases

These case stories together show a troubling reality: child protection and family law too often misunderstand or minimise coercive control. The patterns are apparent:

Children's behaviour is misread. Silence is mistaken for neutrality, resistance for defiance, and rejection of a safe caregiver for alienation. These are survival responses to fear, manipulation, and indoctrination.

People overvalue surface-level functioning. If a child attends school or presents as functioning, agencies may dismiss more profound trauma. People often mistakenly equate the absence of harm with the lack of physical injury.

The report has limitations. Family reports, expert assessments, and child protection case notes often cannot capture patterns of coercive control, instead reducing them to isolated incidents or post-separation conflict.

They reframe protective parents as hostile or suffering from mental health issues because they often present distress due to not feeling heard and trying to protect their child.

Time works in favour of the perpetrator. The longer the proceedings drag on, the more opportunity coercive control has to entrench itself. This can deepen a child's rejection of the safe caregiver and erode secure attachments.

The protective parent often develops mental health issues because of the situation that goes against them. This affects functional capacity to work, among many other areas.


### The Human Cost

Behind each of these cases lies a child learning a devastating lesson: that their voice does not matter, that their safety is negotiable, and that systems cannot always distinguish between love and manipulation.

**"The court thought my child was choosing, but I knew it wasn't their voice; it was the other parents," - the Survivor.**

Another reflected:

**"They said there was no harm because they were still going to school. They didn't see the nightmares, the panic attacks, the way they flinched whenever their phone rang."**

For protective parents, the cost is equally profound: losing the ability to safeguard their children, being blamed for raising concerns, and living with the grief of watching bonds with their children fracture under coercive pressure.

## Why Misinterpretation Happens

These failures do not result from isolated mistakes but from systemic blind spots.

Training for child protection workers, report writers, and Independent Children's Lawyers focuses on law and procedure, not on child development, trauma, or coercive control.

Risk assessments prioritise visible harm, leaving psychological abuse and indoctrination overlooked.

Legal culture treats coercive control as "allegations to be tested," demanding levels of proof that are unrealistic for hidden patterns of abuse.

### Research insight

Mental health effects.
A recent systematic review finds coercive control is associated with PTSD/complex-PTSD and depression (adult survivors, with clear implications for children in these environments). Australian synthesis work

also highlights significant harms to children living with interparental coercive control.

Assessment challenges.
Australian reviews caution that frontline assessments often misread coercive control as "situational" conflict, leading to mismatched responses; distinguishing patterns of coercive control vs. other IPV types is essential in child and family practice. Recent Australian journal work explicitly compares these patterns in child-involved cases.

Practitioner blind spots.
A qualitative study with Australian child-protection practitioners found practitioners overlooked or confused indicators of coercive control with other patterns in case vignettes, which left children under-protected.

Recovery is possible.
Evidence syntheses show that safety, stability, and consistent support (e.g., trauma-informed, caregiver-child work) improve children's outcomes after DFV exposure; systematic reviews increasingly support integrated IPV/VAC responses.

Legal/policy fragmentation.
The Australian Law Reform Commission (ALRC) Report 114 documents fragmentation between family law and child-protection systems, noting risks that family-violence harms, including psychological abuse, do not adequately safeguard children.

Children are direct victims, not bystanders.
Evan Stark's *Children of Coercive Control* (2023, Oxford University Press) synthesises evidence that coercive control is a central context for child abuse and serious developmental harm—children are within coercive regimes.

## From the Therapy Room

In my professional work, I have encountered endless systemic injustices. I have sat with families who have done everything they could to seek safety, only to drown in a system that moves too slowly, costs too much, and sometimes cannot protect the very people it serves.

I referred countless clients to specialist legal support, knowing that without expert help, they could not understand their legal issues. However, the cost of family law proceedings is staggering.

I have collaborated with parents who had to sell their homes to cover the cost of legal fees. Sometimes, Legal Aid offered a grant of help, but only if the client signed an agreement allowing a caveat of an undisclosed amount over the family home. Financial abuse continues under a new name, sanctioned by the very systems meant to help them rebuild.

I have seen the heartbreak when parents cannot afford representation and must stand in court alone, trying to explain coercive control in a system that still demands evidence of bruises.

I have had my heart broken too many times to count by hearing and speaking with people and families who have experienced the impact of suicide after erasers from their children lives, not because they were unsafe parents, but because the process was too long, costly, and crushing for them to endure.

The current child support system is inherently flawed. I have witnessed the perspectives of both the payer and receiver sides of this system. Parents in poverty, while manipulated assessments financially strangled others and weaponised debt collection. The abuse continues through official channels.

I have seen up close so many of the tactics used to control children.

These realities are heartbreaking and infuriating. They have shown me that coercive control is not just about what happens inside one household; it is about systems that allow abuse to continue in alternative forms. Every time I witness a child's safe relationship ruined by manipulation or legal delay, it strengthens my resolve to advocate for change in systems that prioritise their safety and allow children not to carry the weight of adult conflict.

## My journey

I have faced the most horrific and painful experiences imaginable, the kind that nearly broke me. There were nights I wondered if I would survive, and days when fear and exhaustion felt unbearable. I am still here.

Writing this chapter is deeply personal. Each story, each example, reflects not only what I have witnessed professionally but also what I have lived. If you are going through this now, my heart goes out to you. I know how heavy it feels to keep going when every system fails you. All I can say is I send you love.

# Part Three
# Recognising the Tactics

## DARVO

This chapter explores DARVO, a psychological defence pattern often used by perpetrators of harm when confronted. The material may feel confronting, especially if you have experienced gaslighting, coercive control, or other forms of abuse.

Survival does not come with instructions. We invent tools in the moment, not because we want to, but because we must.

When shaping this book, I debated where to place this chapter. It could have come later, after sharing more lived stories and affects, but I brought it forward. The reason is simple: the techniques introduced here — recognising DARVO, setting boundaries, and planning for safety — are easier to understand and apply if you already have the language and awareness.

By learning these concepts now, you will read the chapters that follow with clearer eyes. You will see how people create survival strategies in real-time, and how they utilise tools such as safety planning, self-reflection, and boundary setting in their daily lives.

## Definition and Concept

DARVO is an acronym coined by psychologist Dr Jennifer Freyd in the 1990s. It stands for:

**Deny**

**Attack**

**Reverse Victim and Offender**

It describes a typical pattern used by perpetrators of domestic violence, coercive control, or abuse when confronted. Rather than taking accountability, they deny harm, attack the person raising the issue, and flip the narrative so they appear to be the actual victim.

## Why Perpetrators Use DARVO?

DARVO is not random; it serves a purpose. Whether consciously planned or reflexively used, it is a defence mechanism designed to protect the person from accountability and maintain control.

**Self-protection**: confrontation threatens their image of themselves as reasonable or justified. DARVO enables them to deflect guilt or shame by denying harm and redirecting blame.

**Power Preservation**: Coercive control is all about maintaining dominance. By reversing the roles of victim and offender, the person regains the upper hand and keeps the other person off-balance.

**Credibility Management**: DARVO is effective in coercive control contexts, as it can confuse outsiders, friends, family, professionals, or even the court. This raises doubts about the survivor's credibility and reduces the likelihood of consequences, even for the perpetrator.

## DARVO as Part of Coercive Control

DARVO is not just about defending against one accusation: it is part of the larger pattern of coercive control. When a survivor confronts harm, DARVO can re-establish control by making them question their own memory, feel guilty for speaking up, and withdraw their complaint. This maintains the abusive dynamic, silencing resistance and discouraging future disclosures.

DARVO becomes a well-rehearsed script. Over time, each successful use reinforces the behaviour, making it the default response to any challenge.

## Why DARVO Matters?

DARVO is powerful because it undermines confidence and distorts reality. When used effectively, it can prompt recipients to question their own memories, evoke feelings of guilt or shame, and even deter them from seeking support.

Recognising DARVO can be a turning point. It helps you pause, trust your own experience, and see the behaviour for what it is. Once I learnt about DARVO, I could not unsee the pattern. This was especially clear in written text, where the minimisation, denial and reversal of blame became clear.

## The Psychological Impact of DARVO

DARVO not only confuses, but it can also affect the body and brain. When someone experiences denial, attack, and reversal, their amygdala and HPA axis activate, releasing cortisol and adrenaline.

This can lead to:

Hyperarousal: racing heart, shaking, feeling panicked or angry.

Freeze Response: shutting down, going blank, or going quiet.

Self-doubt: the brain's conflict-monitoring centre (anterior cingulate cortex) activates, leading to rumination and second-guessing.

Shame and Withdrawal: Many survivors retreat after DARVO, which can isolate them and prevent them from seeking help.

## DARVO Can Be Subtle

Not all DARVO is loud or angry. Perpetrators use a softer, quieter version, which can be just as destabilising.

Variations include:

Pity Play: "I cannot believe you would accuse me of that — you know how hard life has been for me."

Over-Compliance: "Fine, I guess I will just never speak to anyone again." (making the survivor feel guilty)

Charm or Love-Bombing: Switching suddenly to compliments or promises can confuse the survivor and make them question whether confrontation was necessary.

## DARVO in Real Life

Understanding DARVO is one thing; recognising it now is something else entirely. The pattern can feel so confusing that you may leave the conversation questioning yourself, your memory, or even your motives.

Let us examine what DARVO sounds like in everyday life, both during a relationship and after separation. Notice that the specific words may change, but the pattern stays the same: first comes denial, then attack, then reversal.

Example 1: Emotional Abuse

You: "It frightened me when you slammed the door so hard last night."
Partner:

DENY: "I did not slam it... the wind caught it."

ATTACK: "You are ridiculous, always blowing things out of proportion."

REVERSE: "You make me lose my temper. If you had not pushed me, I would not have reacted."

Example 2: Public Incident

You: "I felt humiliated when you criticised me in front of your family at dinner."
Partner:

DENY: "I was not criticising... I was joking."

ATTACK: "You are too uptight. Nobody else thought it was important."

REVERSE: "You embarrassed me by sulking afterwards. You ruined the night, not me."

Example 3: Financial Control

You: "I discovered you cancelled my debit card without providing me any notice."

Partner:

DENY: "I did not cancel it... the bank must have made a mistake."

ATTACK: "You are hopeless with money. Someone must take control."

REVERSE: "I am the one carrying the financial burden. You should thank me, not complain."

Example 4: Isolation Tactics

You: "It hurt me when you told my coworker not to invite me to the staff get-together."

Partner:

DENY: "I never said that. You are imagining things."

ATTACK: "Your colleagues do not even like you — I am just protecting you from embarrassment."

REVERSE: "You are the one who leaves me out. I am always alone while you are off with them."

Example 5: Parenting Decisions

You: "I dislike how you shouted at the kids last night. They were frightened.

Partner:

DENY: "I did not shout... I was talking firmly."

ATTACK: "You always undermine me in front of the kids. No wonder they do not respect me."

REVERSE: "You are the one who confuses them by being too soft. I am the only proper parent here."

Example 6: Technology Surveillance

You: "I noticed you have been checking my phone messages."

Partner:

DENY: "I was not checking... I just glanced at the screen when it lit up."

ATTACK: "Why are you so defensive? Must be something you are hiding."

REVERSE: "If you were trustworthy, I would not need to look at all."


Example 7: Work and Career

You: "It hurt me when you told my colleagues I was lazy in front of everyone."

Partner:

DENY: "I never said that... you are twisting my words."

ATTACK: "You cannot even take a joke at work? You are embarrassing."

REVERSE: "If you worked harder, I would not have to say anything at all."


Example 8: Health and Well-being

You: "I would like to go to the doctor about my anxiety."

Partner:

DENY: "You do not need a doctor. You are fine."

ATTACK: "You are wasting money we do not have. You always make everything about yourself".

REVERSE: "You make me anxious with your constant complaining. I am the one who needs help, not you."

Example 9: Seeking Support

You: "I talked to my sister about how stressed I have been lately."
Partner:

DENY: "You did not talk to her about me... You are exaggerating again."

ATTACK: "You are disloyal, running to your family behind my back."

REVERSE: "You are the one ruining this relationship by gossiping. I cannot trust you anymore."

Example 10: Child Support

You: "The child support payment did not come through this week."
Co-Parent:

DENY: "I told you I do not have money right now."

ATTACK: "Are you spying on me? You are so controlling."

REVERSE "You are causing our kid stress."

Example 11: Parenting arrangements

"Our child mentioned feeling scared when your friend shouted at them last weekend."
DENY: "That never happened; they are exaggerating or making it up."

ATTACK: "You are coaching them to say this; you have always tried to turn them against me."

REVERSE: "You are the one damaging their relationship with me by filling their head with lies."

Example 11: Expressing the Desire to Leave

You: "I have been unhappy for a long time, and I think it might be best for us to separate."
Partner:

DENY: "You're not unhappy .... you are just stressed and overthinking everything."

ATTACK: "You are selfish for even saying that. After everything I have done for you, this is how you repay me?"

REVERSE: "You are the one destroying this family... do not blame me when the kids grow up hating you."

## Why This Moment Is So Dangerous?

Leaving a controlling relationship often triggers the highest risk period for escalation. Neuroscience research shows that when a person with poor impulse control feels their power slipping away, the amygdala, the brain's threat centre, can go into overdrive. This can lead to hypervigilance, retaliation, and increased coercion or violence, which is why careful safety planning is essential.

## Why DARVO Hits Hard Post-Separation

DARVO can be even more powerful after separation, as it often unfolds in front of family consultants, mediators, lawyers, or even the court. When the person causing harm uses denial, attack, and reversal effectively, they can appear calm and reasonable while painting the protective parent as "hysterical" or "high conflict."

This can confuse decision-makers, delay protective action, and leave children in unsafe situations. Recognising DARVO helps survivors, practitioners, and systems stay focused on the behaviour, not the blame-shifting.

## How to Respond to DARVO (If Safe)

Prioritise Safety

If you feel unsafe, disengage. Research on coercive control

shows that challenging a perpetrator now can escalate risk, especially during separation.

Your priority is physical and emotional safety, not confrontation.

Recognising DARVO is empowering, but responding requires care. The goal is not to win the argument, but to keep yourself safe, grounded and supported.

If you try to explain further to the perpetrator, the cycle can continue:

Gaslighting/Minimizing: "Things are not so bad ... You are making a big deal out of nothing.

Escalated Attack: "No one else would put up with you. You should be grateful I am still here."

Further Reversal: "You have been impossible to live with. I should be the one leaving you."

Document do not debate.

Evidence from family law practice recommends keeping a written record of incidents (emails, texts, diary notes). Documentation can be crucial for courts, mediators, or child protection professionals to observe the pattern of behaviour over time safely.

Seek External Validation

Discuss your experience with a trusted friend, therapist, or support worker. Research shows that survivors who share their experiences with supportive others are less likely to internalise blame and more likely to seek help.

Professional Support & Safety Planning

Consider consulting a family violence service, lawyer, or support line to discuss next steps and create a safety plan. This is especially important if DARVO escalates to threats, stalking, or violence.

## For Professionals: Responding to DARVO

Professionals in law, social work, or mental health often encounter DARVO in case files, interviews, and even courtrooms. Recognising it is the first step; responding effectively is what prevents harm from being minimised or reframed.

Proven methods for success.

Stay neutral but curious. Document what people say without adopting the narrative of reversal. Naming the shift (e.g. "I notice the focus has moved from the original issue to blame") can disrupt DARVO patterns.

Separate fact from spin. Focus on verifiable events and timelines rather than character attacks. This keeps attention anchored.

Provide validation. Affirm the reporting person's right to raise concerns (e.g. "It is reasonable to talk about safety concerns for the child"). This helps counteract the silencing effect of DARVO.

Keep logical records. Contemporaneous notes are critical. Courts and agencies are more likely to act when people document patterns well.

Invest in training and supervision. Organisations should provide staff training on coercive control, gaslighting, and DARVO, so frontline workers can identify these tactics early and respond consistently.

If you confuse DARVO with a genuine misunderstanding or conflict, remember, DARVO is a pattern, not a one-off disagreement.


## My journey

I had learnt about Darvo years ago, but it was only when someone sat down with me and applied it to my situation that it clicked. Every message that had once made me spiral with guilt or self-doubt suddenly made sense. Someone turned on the light so I could see.

I saw it everywhere — in conversations, in text messages, and even in the way I replayed arguments in my mind. Once I recognised the pattern, my first instinct was to use that knowledge as a tool. I wanted to name it, to hold the other person accountable.

That need for me to tell them I had learned what they had been doing to me — that part of me that longed for justice — I hoped they might finally admit what had been happening. I hoped they would apologise and declare they would try to improve and stop this form of communication.

The reaction I got left me devastated. The perpetrator said I was mentally disturbed. Those words cut deeply, yet they also brought clarity. Their response confirmed what I had been living all along: DARVO was not a onetime tactic; it was the truth of a very unhealthy and abusive relationship.

I had to learn that I could not expect any accountability, so I stopped waiting. Of all the things I had survived — and there are so many — this was the one that changed everything. I could not heal in the same place that was continuously breaking me.

# The Grey Rock Method

## Origins of the Grey Rock Method

Survivor communities developed the Grey Rock Method in the early 2010s as a grassroots strategy for coping with narcissistic abuse and coercive control. The first widely cited description came from a 2012 blog post by a survivor, who wrote under the pseudonym Skylar.

Skylar suggests that when leaving was not immediately possible, survivors could make themselves appear "as boring as a grey rock" to reduce the abuser's attention and control.

From there, the idea spread quickly through survivor forums, domestic violence support groups, and eventually into self-help resources and practitioner literature. Its popularity reflected a truth: survivors often needed practical strategies in situations where traditional systems left them without protection.

Leaving was not an immediate option. Children, finances, community ties, or ongoing legal proceedings made it unavoidable to continue contact with the perpetrator. Formal systems often overlook coercive control, focusing on single incidents of violence instead of the broader pattern of domination. Survivors had to create their own tools to manage these daily interactions.

Grey Rock became one of those tools. It did not depend on the abuser changing or on institutions recognising the harm. Instead, it offered survivors a way to conserve emotional energy, reduce escalation, and regain control over even the smallest moments.

That it emerged from the survivors themselves is significant. Grey Rock is more than a coping technique; it is a testament to the resilience and creativity of survivors in the face of systemic neglect.

## Limits and Risks of the Grey Rock Method

While the Grey Rock Method can be a valuable tool, it is not without limitations and potential risks. It is essential to note that this strategy is not suitable in all situations.

Risk of Escalation
Some perpetrators may notice the survivor's lack of engagement and respond with increased aggression to regain control. Therefore, you should never use Grey Rock if a safety threat is immediate, unless it is part of a larger safety plan.

Emotional Toll on Survivors
Deliberately shutting down natural responses can be exhausting. Survivors may feel silenced or invisible when they cannot express themselves. Over time, this can take a heavy emotional toll. Grey Rock works best as a short-term tool rather than a long-term way of relating.

Limited Scope
Grey Rock does not stop abuse. It cannot replace protective measures such as legal orders, professional support, or leaving an unsafe environment. It is simply a strategy for managing specific interactions, often when complete disengagement is not yet possible.

Not Universally Appropriate
Survivors, especially those living with elevated levels of trauma or dissociation, may find it challenging to

keep up the neutral stance Grey Rock requires. In such cases, attempting to use it without support may increase stress instead of reducing it.

## Variations and Alternatives

Because every situation of coercive control is unique, the Grey Rock Method is not the only available option. Survivors and practitioners have adapted it into variations that are more suitable for specific contexts.

## The Yellow Rock Method

Explicitly developed for co-parenting and family court situations, Yellow Rock is a gentler alternative to Grey Rock. Instead of appearing cold or dismissive, survivors communicate politely and respectfully, keeping their responses brief. The tone is "warm" enough to satisfy professionals who may monitor communication, while still protecting the survivor from conflict.

For example, a parent might respond with: "Thank you for your message. I will confirm the school pickup at 3 pm."

This also maintains boundaries and prevents others from perceiving them as uncooperative, potentially using it against survivors in legal disputes.

## No Contact

The most effective boundary, when safe and possible, is to cut off all communication with the perpetrator. This may include blocking phone numbers, emails, and social media, as well as avoiding shared spaces. However, for survivors, particularly those with children or financial ties, a complete lack of contact is not realistic.

## Low Contact
A middle ground, often necessary in co-parenting arrangements, is "low contact." Communication focuses on practical matters, such as children's needs. Parents often use structured methods, such as parenting apps or email templates. Low contact reduces the abuser's access to the survivor's emotions while keeping communication channels open where required.

## Parallel Strategies
Grey Rock, Yellow Rock, No Contact, or Low Contact are most effective when combined with other strategies such as safety planning, trauma-informed counselling, and community or legal support. Survivors can use these tools to manage high-risk or unavoidable interactions immediately, rather than relying solely on them.

## Gentle note
If Grey Rock or its variations do not feel safe or possible for you, that does not mean you are failing. It means your situation requires a different approach. Every survivor's journey is unique, and safety is always the top priority. Support, resources, and belief matter most.

## Everyday Conversations
These are flat, non-engaging responses that avoid over-explaining or defending.

## Everyday Examples

Perpetrator: "Why are you so quiet? Are you hiding something?"
Grey Rock Response: "I am fine."

Perpetrator: "What did you do all day? Must have been something lazy."
Grey Rock Response: "Nothing much."

Perpetrator: "The kids like me better. You are a terrible parent."
Grey Rock Response: "Pickup is at 3 pm."

Perpetrator: "You will find no one else."
Grey Rock Response: "That is your opinion."

## Simple Grey Rock Sentences

"Okay."

"I see."

"Noted."

"That is your opinion."

"If you say so."

"Nothing much."

"Sure."

"No."

## What breaks Grey Rock?

Grey Rock loses its power if you slip into:

Over-explaining, "I swear I was not cheating; I was only at the store for 20 minutes."

Defending, "That is not fair. I am a good parent."

Justifying, "I only dressed up because of work, not for attention."

Arguing back, "You are the one who never helps around here!"

False apologising: "I am sorry you think that; I will try harder."

## From the Therapy Room

I once supported a client who felt like every conversation was an interrogation. Even simple questions like, "What did you do today?" turned into a cross-examination. They said it was like being on a witness stand 24/7.

We explored ways to save their emotional energy. As a small experiment, they tried Grey Rock: instead of defending or over-explaining, they used short, neutral answers, such as "It was fine" or "Not much." They joke it was like turning into a "boring TV channel no one wanted to watch." Over time, they noticed arguments were shorter, and they left those interactions less drained. Grey Rock did not change the abuser's behaviour overall, but it gave them back a small sense of choice in moments where they had felt powerless.

Another client tried Grey Rock during a high-risk period. At first, the arguments seemed to ease, but the abuser quickly noticed something was different. Neutrality was defiance: "Why are you being cold? What are you hiding?" The result was an outburst of violence.

This highlighted an important lesson: Grey Rock can be a helpful tool, but it is not a magic shield. In some situations, it may reduce conflict; in others, it may escalate risk. Like any strategy, it works best when paired with safety planning and support.

## When They Move on but Do not Let Go.

Another tricky thing survivors face is watching how quickly the perpetrator moves on to a new relationship. I have repeatedly seen that the abuser cannot fuel themselves with the survivor's emotions when the survivor sets boundaries and employs protective methods. Instead, they seem to move on overnight, finding someone else to meet their needs, all while continuing to harass, stalk, or try to pull the survivor back in.

This can be deeply confusing and painful. Survivors describe feeling as though their entire world had shattered, while the abuser replaces them without pause.

This is another pattern of coercive control:

Securing a fresh supply: When cut off from one person's emotions, attention, or resources, they often seek another to meet those needs.

Maintaining control: Even while involved with someone else, there can be ongoing harassment or contact with their former partner. This is not about love; it is about keeping control.

Using the new relationship as a tool, perpetrators even draw the new partner into the abuse, sharing confidential information, spreading misinformation, or using them to monitor, stalk, or harass the survivor. This can deepen the sense of intrusion and make it seem impossible to maintain boundaries.

Punishing independence: Moving on quickly can deliberately wound, confuse, or punish the survivor for leaving or not meeting their needs.

Recognising this pattern helps reduce self-blame. Their behaviour is not a reflection of the survivor's worth, but of their ongoing need for control and supply. As painful as it feels, their ability to move on is not proof that you were unlovable. It is a tactic and another reminder of why your boundaries matter.

## Research insight

Coercive control depends not only on physical dominance but on provoking emotional reactions. Perpetrators use intimidation, guilt-tripping, gaslighting, and DARVO strategies to elicit fear, anger, or self-doubt, keeping survivors entrapped in cycles of control (Stark, 2007; Bancroft, 2002).

The Grey Rock Method aims to disrupt this cycle. By presenting as emotionally neutral, survivors deny perpetrators the "fuel" of emotional reactivity. Behavioural psychology explains this mechanism: according to conditioning principles, behaviours that are not reinforced decrease over time (Skinner, 1953/1999). When manipulation no longer produces visible distress or drama, the incentive to persist in that tactic can weaken.

Neuroscience underscores the value of such strategies. Survivors often live with a sensitised stress response, where the amygdala triggers fight, flight, or freeze even in low-level conflict. Trauma research highlights how chronic coercive control conditions the nervous system into hypervigilance (van der Kolk,

2014). Grey Rock can function as a deliberate form of emotional regulation—conserving energy, reducing reactivity, and interrupting the abuser's reward cycle.

## Gentle note

No one knows this person better than you do. You have already developed strategies that have carried you through impossible situations. You are the expert of your own survival.

The tools here are not rules; they are options. Take what strengthens you; leave what does not. Trust the wisdom you have already built. Your instincts, your strategies, and your strength are the foundation. These are just additional tools to complement the ones you already possess.

# Part Four
# Voices of Lived Experience

## "I believed I was going crazy."

This diary contains personal reflections on coercive control, sexual coercion, and emotional abuse.
Readers may find this content triggering. Please take care of yourself as you read. In Australia, you can call 1800RESPECT (1800 737 732) for 24/7 confidential help. If you are in immediate danger, please call 000.

### A Note on Memory and Trauma

The survivor originally wrote and emailed these diary entries when they felt like they were going crazy. Gaslighting was constant; reality itself felt uncertain. Writing became a way to capture truth now — a lifeline when memory later blurred or shut down.

For a long time, trauma's protective fog was buried, and cycles of love bombing blurred these events. When they re-read the emails years later, the memories resurfaced piece by piece, revealing the reality that people had minimised, denied, or erased.

This diary is not just a memory. It is evidence of survival amid gaslighting. It shows how trauma can silence, distort, and conceal.

## Diary Entries

28 April
I have been trying to put in boundaries, but I do not feel supported or respected. Right before an important call, it became about them again. When I tried to say no, they would not listen. That day, I found out words had been spread about me to others. Those people told me directly they felt it was emotional abuse.

29 April
While I was at work, a visitor came to the house, trying to convince me to stay in the relationship. I was honest about the drinking and felt drained.

1 May
There were sexual advances I did not want. My "no" was ignored. I felt trapped in my home and body.

2 May
Lies are being told about me, even to my family. I tried to hold boundaries and say it was time to move out, but the pressure for sex continued. Against my will, I ended up complying out of fear and exhaustion.

3 May
Talk of houses, future-faking rules, and conditions of "breaks." I was told I was not acting morally, that I needed a doctor. I slept in another room; in the middle of the night, my boundaries were ignored. Porn was put on, and sex happened without my consent. I was told I had "enjoyed it"

4 May
Calls came in about making doctors' appointments

"for us." Promises of support, of love, of being together. Talk of matching pyjamas, journeys, building futures, and marriage. Long declarations about working on things together, about mental health, about love that is undeniable. I listened, mostly silent, as the words kept coming.

By the end of the call, I felt drained, silenced, and manipulated. I could barely get a word in. My boundaries are not respected again. I am doubting myself, questioning my sanity. I try to tell myself: this is about control, about keeping me from leaving, even after I have said it's over clearly.

I paid for the accommodation to create distance. I do not know what to expect next, but I know I am scared. Writing this down is my way of holding on to the truth.

10:41 am, 4 May
I send this to myself now, as proof, as record, as prayer.

# Inside the Rollercoaster: Two Weeks in Messages

A survivor's sharing-

We could fix it. Maybe if I said the right thing or stayed calm, things would settle. These are messages from just two weeks. When I looked back months later, I realised how unpredictable every single day was: love, rage, apology, blame, all in the same breath.

Week One

**Monday**

"You do not even realise how much you are hurting me and destroying me."
"I have done nothing wrong. I love you, and that is it."

**Tuesday**

"Babe, are you okay? You are worrying me."
"Babe, you are not answering your phone."
"Are you okay???"
"Babe, I am worried. Pick up your phone."
"What time is your test?"
"You should stay off Bumble."

**Wednesday**

"More deflection. No accountability. Just answer my question?"
"Do not hang up on me again. Answer your phone now."
"Babe, I only want the best for you. I struggle when I am jealous. I want to marry you."

**Thursday**

"I just cannot believe you. I am trying to build a future with you."

"I do not want to be involved with your friends."

"You are acting shady. You are self-destructing."

**Friday**

"All I need is you. I love you so much. Please, you are my everything."

"I cannot cope anymore. I am not joking. All I want to do is

stay in bed and cry."

"Hey, babe, I really need you right now."

**Saturday**

"You have broken me, and I did not need this. Trust me."

"I just had the worst panic attack ever 😵."

"I just smashed the car."

**Sunday**

"I cannot live without you anymore. I will do everything it takes to be better. How can I have my stuff picked up?" Love you, and I care about you more than anything"

Week 2

**Monday**

"How come you got your location off? Shady.""""" bet if I drive up to your house, they will be there. I'll see you soon 😈.""" Thanks for giving me all the anxiety. You made it ten times worse."

Tuesday.

I always do everything without thinking about anybody else, especially me. I am disappointed

😦 😦 😦.""""" me really — do you think I am going to read this shit? you are a joke."

### Wednesday

I am taking a break in our relationship now. I need to take a breath and pick myself up.

I am going to my family. I sent you the plane ticket to show you I am not lying.

You have broken me. I just wanted to marry you.

### Thursday

Silence ----- I am feeling abandoned and panicked; they have really left me.

### Friday

Good morning, sweetheart.

I miss you so much I cannot live without you. I am going to book air tickets and would like to fly up ASAP.

Being away from you is breaking my heart and spirit. I need you; you need me.

I can no longer live without you. I will do everything it takes to be a better person.

Why can't you understand I love you so much, I will do everything it takes?

If you need an excuse to cheat, go for it; you have got it.

Help me rebuild it. I love you very much.

### Saturday

When I did not respond after these, I received this.

I do not think you have had my best interests at heart for a long time. I love you, but I have high expectations, and if I am honest, you cannot meet them. You never did. I will not live like this.

My heart broke here. I remember thinking, 'I am not good enough... they do not want me.' I thought about all the things I could have done to be good enough. I felt like I had been a poor partner.

They contacted my friend, who lived in another state, to convince them that they are so concerned about me and my mental health, and that I do not know how to be loved, that I was unstable, as I am jeopardising the relationship and pushing away the only person who loves and cares for me. My friend told me they really loved me and that I should try with them. The people who live near me reminded me that there was nothing wrong with me. They had manipulated my friend, who is in another state, as they could not manipulate the surrounding people, so I snapped.

Me

You need to stay away from me. You are unstable and scaring me — it is over!!!
Your behaviour towards me is disgusting.
The police will be here. I have had enough. You do not stop.
I have deleted the location app. We are done.

Everything in me wanted to defend myself. For years, I had

sacrificed for them, always trying to put their best interests at heart, but they never heard me or saw me. My value was always in question. I felt dismissed as unworthy, and I can never meet their shifting expectations.

After I tried to set the boundaries, I was terrified of losing them. I feared they would abandon me, believing I had made the biggest mistake. I just wanted them. They did not end up listening, and the pattern continued for longer. I got stuck in the hoovering—the concept of where the abuser sucked me back into the relationship.

Months later, I realised the two-week pattern was a weekly pattern of accusations, apologies, begging, blame, looping like a broken record. I kept thinking I could fix it if I tried harder, but it never changed. If I had not answered the phone, they would have shown up at my house. They watched me. They stalked me.

Eventually, the weight broke me. My body and mind could no longer carry it. When the police finally intervened, I begged them not to......, but now I am grateful they did not listen.

**Gentle note:** Feeling heartbroken in these moments is entirely normal. The pain runs deep because it clashes with our values, our desire to love, to be loyal, to be seen as "enough." That heartbreak does not make us weak; it shows just how human, caring, and deeply invested we were.

# Through a Friend's Eyes:

This sharing is of a friend of a person who witnessed coercive control behaviours/

The friend shared they knew something was not right within the relationship yet were not aware that everything was the behaviours that made up coercive control. Still, with the benefit of hindsight and education, they are now aware of it.

"I have known B for approximately two years, and the former partner, X, for about half that time. X initially seemed quite normal, even dull: charming, funny and friendly, and B seemed in love and happy. To the outside, all was well; X and B seemed happy.

B laughs without prompting, smiles and has an infectious zest for life, admired by many people. However, after spending more time in each other's company, this façade unraveled for them both.

B's light seemed to dim gradually; B shrank as if being slowly deflated, and the person I knew and loved was fading away. There was no spontaneous laughter anymore; B seemed edgy, nervous, and constantly checking their phone.

If X was not with B they were constantly being phoned by X, questioned as to B whereabouts, and no time spent with B did not include them. The friendship became quite uncomfortable for a time because of this, and I was the problem when I tried to talk to B about X always being with B

Once, the gentle handholding of a couple in love became a constant hold on B. In company and social situations, X always had a hand on B. When B tried to pull away, X dragged B closer. I could tell B was uncomfortable but did not know how to voice it.

At family gatherings and in front of B closest friends, X belittled B, put B down, and laughed at B I could see how

much this hurt B, and it absolutely broke my heart that I did not know how to comfort B. There was never time, because X was always there, always watching B phone. It was a burden I had to bear on my own, with no tools, no label for the behaviours, and no idea how to help. I felt powerless.

X also restricted B movement by using B car to commute to X work, effectively rendering B housebound in a regional community. Cut off family, friends, and social opportunities.

After B told X to move out, the control did not stop. In fact, it intensified. X tried to manipulate me personally by spreading misinformation about B and impugning their character. It was disgusting and still affects me mentally to this day. Observers often misunderstand or disregard its effect.

I have seen one of my closest, dearest friends being under surveillance, on edge, in tears constantly and manipulated by this person, which continues to this day.

Even after moving out, X turned up randomly at B home, and I was in the middle of several shouting matches and anger that had a marked psychological effect.

My heart absolutely broke and still does for my friend. That is why I am so bloody proud of the amazing, strong, beautiful, passionate person they are.

If only I had had tools or words at the time to help her identify coercive control, I could have prevented some of the suffering.

# Many Masks: The Phone as a Leash.

Since leaving the relationship, the survivor revisits messages and moments to write this chapter and identify patterns.

The night began with fear. Without consent, the perpetrator barged in instantly, shifting blame.

**Them.**

Are you and your mate going to throw me under a bus?

I am absolutely petrified... It is five years in jail. No suspended sentences. Straight up. Done.

Because I do not want to go to jail, do you really want to have a rant? I know, and I am the one who is going to sit in jail. And you will not give a fuck. Think about that.

(This was not about accountability. It was about making me feel responsible for their choices.

I tried to ask about drinking. The answer turned into excuses, complaints, and circular arguments.

Me - Have you been drinking tonight? I want you to be honest with me.

**Them** - Yeah, I have had a couple... but I cannot afford to be there. What is the point of paying $550 a week for a tiny place with nothing? I cannot even get Netflix!

(Even when I pointed out the truth that the internet worked, they denied it, repeating themselves until I gave up).

The Child in the Crossfire:

When I stood firm about my child, they twisted it into a money issue. Me- I will not stand down. I will not stand down for my child.
**Them:** It is just wasting time and money. It will not solve anything. I want to move forward and buy a house. Even parenting became about them.

False Vulnerability:

When I finally asked them to leave, the mask slipped again. **Them**: I came all the way here just because I needed a cuddle. I do not have anyone else.

This was not tenderness. It was pressure in another way to make me feel guilty for saying no.


Love-Bombing:

Them: After Conflict - Babe, I really want to talk to you today, okay? I have a surprise for you.

Future-faking:

**Them**: In Japan, exactly 4 weeks today - wow, cannot wait. Hey, what are you doing next Sunday? I have tickets.


Performative Accountability:

I can own my mistakes and strive to improve... I know I am not perfect, but no one is.


Shifting blame:

Me- What about the intent and manipulation?
**Them:** You asked for all my bank accounts... I do not even understand what you are talking about.

Financial Deception & Control:

**Them**: The reason I did not want you to look at the bank was that there was a holiday there, and I wanted it to be a surprise.

Guilt-Tripping & Urgency:

**Them:** I have sent you everything I have, and I am incredibly frustrated because I feel like I am doing everything wrong. Call me.

Jealousy as Surveillance:

**Them:** Why do I feel you are f***ing [friend]? My intuition is telling me this.

Health, Guilt & Emotional Blackmail:

**Them**: I could have another stroke... please appreciate and respect.
I have not slept... all I can do is gag and throw up... I need your help.

I hope you are happy with yourself; you have made me sick... I cannot even go to work because of you.

Gaslighting & Denial:

**Them**: Sorry, I am hiding f**ken nothing... snap out of it... I love you.

Reverse Victim & DARVO – **Them**: You have lied to me, and I know you have cheated. I do not trust you ... You need to take some accountability.

Boundary Violations

Me: Stay away

**Them**: Okay, I will see you soon. This is just stupid.

Boundaries Ignored:

Me- don't feel like talking.

**Them**- Cool, still, babe, sitting. Good morning, what are you doing today?

Sexual Pressure:

**Them:** Babe, I am so horny for you right now.

Comparisons & Triangulation:

**Them**: And I am nothing like your ex-partner and never will be.

Threats of Abandonment & Self-Harm:

**Them:** Trust me; you will never see me again. I have nearly killed myself three times due to all the hurt you have caused me. You are lucky I am even still here.

## Seeing the Pattern

People could dismiss these messages as bad days, misunderstandings, or even love on their own. However, together, they reveal a simple pattern: coercive control.

Love-bombing, guilt, denial, blame-shifting, sexual pressure, and relentless pursuit are not love. They are tools of control, designed to overwhelm and isolate.

For survivors, recognising the pattern is the first step to freedom. For others, these messages are a textbook example of what coercive control sounds like in everyday life.

## Reflection From the Survivor

Looking back through the texts, I can see the masks more clearly. Each message felt separate: an argument, an apology, a demand, a plea. When I read them all together, I see it as a pattern. This is what coercive control looks like in digital form.

Text messages are one of the most potent tools of coercive control because they are constant, instant, and inescapable. The phone becomes a leash:

It is a way to check where I am. It is a way to push through boundaries when I said no. It is a way to demand attention at all hours. It is a way of rewriting reality one line at a time.

## Hope, love, resilience and grace

My name is Cara, and I am a survivor.

The journey was long, painful, and very violent. I am me and I matter, just like the rest of you.

I have dedicated my life to humanity; the service of love; social justice, integrity, grace, and compassion. This is my moral code I live by. I learned it early, and it has failed me a few times, but strangely, it has always been beside me as I have traversed the pits I have been in. I have many women to thank in my life, all of whom I know personally. And I must share that I had a lucky day and finally met a man who is deserving of me.

HOPE exists as does the light of love. Healing is hard; be kind, you are worth it; YOU MATTER

**A Story Untold**

## Grief

Winces of the heart
Emotional dissolution
Endless seconds
Of meaningless
Moments that rule
Our human world
Will the sadness end?
For the moment
It seems never,
lapsing into
Endless notions
the mind unclear
Life will renew
Again
There will be joy
Excitement, love and gratitude
For now, grief
A state of being
Endless

## 2020 Magic- Hope, grace, and compassion

Passion and protection, imbued with integrity and healing, arise.

Leading, loving and living with my loyal pack,
Fully embracing uncensored belief and truth.
Surrendering to the roaring fire of the phoenix
Rising to protect and resting to renew.
All that was loved, lost, or broken on the way.
Creating a solid rock of justice, protection, and courage.
A renewed sense of integrity, vulnerability and fortitude has emerged.
Despair and hopelessness have diminished to ashes, and the ember of self-worth has risen. There are no more secrets to slay.
I am reborn free and wild, rising from the ashes with the gifts of integrity, truth, love and protection.
I am Elcato and Eagle White, the white wolf.

I offer my allegiance to the renewal and rising of the phoenix.

In solidarity, we stand and move together as one.

All my love, forever and true; we all matter
Cara

# Part Five
# Breaking Free & Building Insight

## "But I Love Them" — The Challenge of Loving the Perpetrator:

One of the most brutal truths for survivors to comprehend is that love can exist alongside abuse. Bonded to the person causing harm through shared history, children, financial ties, or fragile hope that things could change. Violence does not erase love; instead, it becomes tangled with fear, obligation, and control.

**"I loved them. That was real. Even when the abuse was real, too."**
**-Survivor.**

This love creates deep confusion. Survivors ask themselves: How can I love someone who hurts me? Does this make me complicit? Am I foolish? That inner conflict feeds shame, as if the very act of loving were evidence of weakness.

Love is not a weakness. Abusers deliberately nurture dependence and attachment, offering tenderness, apologies, and fleeting moments of connection to bind survivors more tightly. This is not blind loyalty, but trauma bonding: a survival response to unpredictable swings between harm and affection.

So often, what survivors ache to hear is human and straightforward: I am sorry. I love you as much as I say I do. I will do anything it takes to become the person you deserve me to be. However, consistent, genuine action must follow those words to be effective. Without action, apologies become another tool of harm —a cycle of empty promises that keep survivors hoping for change that never materialises.

For survivors, the deepest longing is for accountability. Not just for safety, but for truth and an honest acknowledgement from the person causing the harm, such as admitting they were wrong or taking some responsibility. We wait for apologies that never come, and for justice systems that rarely deliver more than fragments.

The truth is this: many people who choose abusive behaviours also decide not to be accountable for their actions. They minimise, deny, or twist the story. They hold on tightly to control because letting it go means facing the weight of their actions. Survivors then carry the silence, the pain of the abuse, and the emptiness of an apology that may never come.

Naming this truth matters. Loving does not make survivors naïve or weak. What demands scrutiny is not their love, but the perpetrators' choice to exploit it.

## The Nature of Accountability

Accountability is more than saying sorry. It is the full-bodied act of owning one's actions, taking responsibility, repairing harm, and committing to change. For survivors, accountability can bring a sense of validation. The perpetrator can show the survivor what happened and acknowledge their responsibility, restoring truth to experiences that were denied.

The opposite is much more common. Perpetrators deploy denial, minimisation, or DARVO, denying, attacking, and reversing roles so they appear the victim. Instead of accountability, survivors encounter blame: "If you had not pushed me, I would not have reacted."

**Barriers to Accountability**

**Why is accountability so rare? The reason is multifaceted.**

Shame is heavy; the only way to escape it is through denial. Others may feel entitled, convinced their control is justified. Narcissism, fear of consequences, and the desire to maintain power can all hinder personal responsibility.

For those with strong narcissistic traits, accountability threatens the very image they work so hard to maintain. To admit harm would mean exposing vulnerability, weakness, or imperfections. Instead, they protect their self-image at all costs, even if it means rewriting history or blaming the survivor. This is not an inability to see reality; it is a refusal to face the discomfort that comes with it.

Narcissism thrives on control, admiration, and the illusion of superiority. Taking accountability undermines all three. Admitting I was wrong breaks the illusion of superiority. To say "I will change" requires surrendering control. In this way, accountability feels more dangerous to them than the abuse itself, so they double down, defend, and deny.

Accountability would require not only words but humility, vulnerability, and sustained change, qualities abusers are unwilling to cultivate. For survivors, understanding this can bring a sense of clarity. It shows why apologies, when they do come, may be shallow, manipulative, or followed quickly by excuses.

## Can narcissists or sociopaths change?

Professionally, in most separation counselling sessions I have facilitated, someone will describe the other as "a narcissist." People use this term so often that it raises an important question: What is a true narcissist?

Narcissism exists on a spectrum. People show narcissistic traits such as selfishness and a lack of empathy in moments of stress and conflict. However, diagnosed narcissistic personality disorder (NPD) is far less common, affecting around 1% of the population. Similarly, experts estimate that antisocial personality disorder (ASPD), which is how sociopathy is more formally diagnosed, affects between 1 and 4% of the population.

This distinction matters. Traits do not always equal a disorder. Survivors still deal with the impact of harmful behaviours, even if they do not meet a clinical threshold.

Can people with strong narcissistic and/or sociopathic traits ever truly change? In theory, yes, change is possible, but only with deep self-awareness, genuine accountability for one's actions, and long-term therapy.

Why It Is Difficult: Denial and defence, narcissists protect their self-image at all costs. To admit harm is to admit imperfection, which feels intolerable. Clinicians often describe sociopathy as antisocial personality disorder characterised by a lack of empathy and remorse, which makes any accountability meaningless.

Both narcissistic and sociopathic personalities blame others: "It is your fault I did this," and externalise blame.

This makes change unlikely, because the first step is accepting responsibility.

Genuine change only happens when someone wants it. Some abusers do not feel a need to change, primarily if control benefits them, or society enables them.

Often, the only time they attempt to change is when there are consequences (e.g. court orders, loss of relationship). However, this supposed change rarely lasts.

Narcissistic and antisocial traits are among the hardest to treat.

Therapy can reduce harmful behaviours, but only if there is consistent engagement, genuine motivation, and strict accountability conditions.

We live in a culture that often excuses or normalises coercive control. Comments like "relationships are hard" or "everyone fights" minimise abuse and shield perpetrators from scrutiny. Communities can silence and stigmatise, discouraging survivors from speaking out. Social myths such as "staying means it cannot have been that bad" unfairly shift blame back onto victims. These cultural narratives allow abusers to continue unchecked, thus reinforcing the idea that accountability is optional rather than essential.

## Choice

Accountability is a choice; it requires someone to confront themselves, an option not taken by all. Denial is still a choice. Some perpetrators choose to continue addictive behaviour as a way of avoiding responsibility. They may blame alcohol, drugs, or gambling for their actions, but these are not the root cause; they are tools of avoidance. Addiction can intensify harmful behaviour, but it does not create abuse. Accountability means recognising both the behaviour and the choices behind it.

While genuine cognitive impairments or disabilities can sometimes affect a person's awareness, most perpetrators of coercive control show clear comprehension. They carefully choose when and where to act, often hiding their behaviour from outsiders. Abuse is not about an inability to understand; it is a choice.

They could control themselves in front of others, so I knew they understood exactly what they were doing. Their choices were not about me, but about themselves.

Most importantly, their refusal to be accountable does not mean there is something wrong with you. It does not mean you are unlovable, undeserving, or at fault. Their choices are theirs alone; your worth is intact.

## How Long Do You Give Someone to Change?

Survivors often ask: "How long do I wait? How many chances do I give?" We do not measure change in weeks, months, or even years. Change requires consistent action.

The actual change is visible. It is not words, promises, or apologies. It is a pattern of accountability, respect, and safety that lasts.

If change is genuine, you will see it early. The first sign is responsibility without excuses: "I hurt you; it was wrong, and here is what I am doing to ensure it never happens again."

If you are still waiting years later, you are living in a cycle.

There is no "right" number of chances, but here is a truth to hold on to: you do not owe unlimited waiting to someone unwilling to be accountable. Every survivor may draw a line and say, "Enough. My healing cannot wait for your transformation."

As one survivor put it:

**"I gave them years, hoping they would finally see what they were doing. All I saw were more excuses. In the end, I realised the only change I could count on was my own."**

## Grief: Mourning What Was and What Never Was

For survivors, grief is one of the most painful yet least spoken-about parts of the healing journey. It is not only grief for the relationship itself but also for everything that surrounded it:

Love you had or still have

A parent you hoped your child would have. The family you never had.

A future you so desperately wanted to build.

Grief here complicates matters. People are grieving not only for what they lost but also for what never truly existed. My dear friend describes grief as an unwelcome visitor.

Survivors often grieve the dream of safety, stability, or family life that was promised but never realised. You may mourn the kind words that came between the cruelty, the version of them you glimpsed only in fleeting moments, or the "what could have been".

Grief often comes in cycles. Survivors may move through the stages of denial, anger, bargaining, sadness, and acceptance: sometimes in a single day. Denial might sound like: "It was not all bad, maybe I exaggerated." Bargaining might whisper: "If I change, maybe they will too." Anger may erupt: "How could they destroy everything we had?" Sadness settles in as you realise the apology may never come, the parent your child deserves may never show up, and the relationship was not what it seemed.

This grief is not weakness. It is a measure of the love you gave, the hope you carried, and the future you longed for. As one survivor said:


**"I was not just grieving the person. I was grieving the dream of us and the parent my child deserved."**

## How does one accept?

Acceptance is not something that happens in a single moment; it can unfold slowly, sometimes painfully.

It does not mean excusing the behaviour, forgiving the harm, or pretending it was less damaging than it was. How does one accept? Facing reality instead of waiting for "maybe"

Acceptance begins when you stop bargaining with hope. "Maybe they will change; maybe this time will be different."

It means choosing to look at the pattern, not the promise.

People must mourn what they lost and what never was to achieve acceptance. Grief becomes an integral part of the process.

Separating self-worth from their choices. Redirecting energy inward means asking: What do I need right now? What is within my power?

Acceptance is not passive. It is an active, courageous step: choosing to stop waiting for their transformation and beginning your own.

As one survivor said:

**"The day I stopped asking why they would not change was the day I changed myself."**

## What Can I Control, and What Can't I Control?

A key step in acceptance recognises the difference between what is within your control and what is not. This distinction can bring clarity and peace, even in the most painful situations.

### What I Cannot Control:

If the other person admits what they did.

They apologise or show remorse.

They changed their behaviour.

How others view the relationship or the abuser.

The justice system's decisions or delays.

The friends and family's opinion or defending the perpetrator

### What I Can Control:

How I respond to other people's choices.

These are the boundaries I set to protect myself and or my children.

Where I place my time, energy, and attention.

Who I allow into my support circle.

The story I tell myself shifts from blame to truth: "This was not my fault.

My healing journey includes therapy, journaling, rest, creativity, and community.

Acceptance does not erase the pain of what you cannot control, but it strengthens your hold on what you can. Each choice you make for yourself, no matter how small, is reclaiming your power.

**"I realised I could not make them change. But I could change my story and start a new chapter" – Survivor.**

## The Pattern of Choice

Abuse is not an accident. It is a pattern of choices that controls, harms, and silences. When perpetrators refuse accountability, that too is a choice, as is choosing denial, attacking instead of reflecting, and continuing in the same cycle.

Survivors can make different choices. Acceptance allows us to step outside that cycle. Instead of tying our healing to their decisions, we tie it to our own. The decision to live free, build safety, reclaim power, and be accountable to us and those we love.

## My journey

When I reflect on accountability now, I realise how much of my energy once went into hoping for change. I longed for them to validate me, to acknowledge what had happened, and to show even a flicker of insight into the harm that they had caused. Instead, I found myself trapped in the waiting: waiting for the apology, waiting for the change, waiting for them to become the person I believed they could be.

Those hopes kept me tethered. I wanted things to work so badly that I convinced myself the failure was mine. I told myself I was not patient enough, loving enough, forgiving enough. I tried harder, loved deeper, and blamed myself for their behaviour.

In my search to make sense of it all, I turned to labels. I read about narcissism, watched videos, and took online quizzes — as if naming the pattern might somehow heal the pain. For a while, it comforted me. It let me believe there was an explanation that could make everything make sense.

"They went through this," I told myself. "They have that condition. It is okay. Love is unconditional." I used to understand it as a shield against the truth, mistaking empathy for obligation. However, love that requires you to shrink, silence, or erase yourself is not love it is survival. I still grieve the future I imagined, the family moments I thought we would share, the person they were. Grief does not follow logic; it comes in waves. Sometimes it is a fleeting memory, other times, it is a heaviness that settles in quietly.

However, alongside the grief, there is acceptance. Acceptance does not erase pain, but it changes the way I carry it. I have learned to hold my story differently, not as a wound, but as wisdom. I choose to turn pain into purpose so that others might recognise themselves in my words and know they are not alone.

Another person's refusal to take responsibility does not define my worth, and it does not make me accountable for what they denied.... It was really a long process for me; I sat in the bargaining stage for a long time. We are all different, and there is no correct way here

## Your turn for self-reflection

Take a moment to pause and reflect. You may like to write your answers in a journal, discuss them with a trusted friend or therapist, or sit quietly with them. There are no right or wrong responses; this is about your truth.

Accountability

What would genuine accountability look like to me?

Have I been waiting for words or actions that may never come?

Barriers

What excuses have I heard most often (denial, blame, addiction, culture)?

How did those excuses affect the way I saw myself?

Labels vs. behaviour

Have I wondered if they are a "narcissist" or "sociopath"?

Does the label matter as much as the impact of their behaviour on me?

Grief

What am I grieving most — the person, the dream, the parent my child deserved, or the future I imagined?

How can I permit myself to feel that grief without shame?

Acceptance and control

What is within my control right now?

What is outside of my control that I need to let go of?

How can I redirect my energy toward my healing and future?

Where would you like to be a year from now?

# The barriers within

Leaving an abusive relationship is not a simple choice; it is one of the most dangerous and complex moments in a survivor's life. Research shows that the risk of homicide or severe harm spikes when a survivor attempts to separate, because leaving directly threatens the abuser's control. What may appear from the outside as an act of freedom is, in the eyes of a perpetrator, a direct challenge to their power.

Beyond this immediate danger lie layers of psychological, social, financial, and systemic barriers that can make leaving feel impossible. Trauma bonds, fear, shame, and dependency all tighten the trap.

## Trauma Bonding and Co-dependency

We will explore trauma bonds soon. They are powerful emotional attachments formed through cycles of fear and intermittent kindness. Survivors may feel pulled back toward the abuser by apologies, promises, or fleeting moments of tenderness. What feels like love from the inside is really survival conditioning, the nervous system clinging to whatever relief it can find.

Alongside this, survivors also develop patterns of co-dependency. This occurs when self-worth becomes tied to meeting the other person's needs, maintaining peace, or resolving their problems. They might believe: if I love them enough, they will change. This belief can make it incredibly hard to step back, because leaving feels like abandoning not only the relationship but also their own sense of purpose and identity.

Trauma bonding and co-dependency create a powerful trap: the body craves connection with the abuser, while the mind believes the survivor must stay, help, and endure. Breaking free requires unravelling the recognition that the pull is not proof of love, and sacrifice does not measure worth.

## Cognitive Dissonance: Loving and Hurting at the Same Time

Survivors can hold two opposing truths at once. This person hurts me, yet they claim to love me. The tension between these truths is unbearable. To survive it, the brain works overtime to make the pieces fit. This often means bending reality to preserve hope. "It is not that bad." "I should not have provoked them."

These thoughts ease the immediate tension, but they also deepen the trap. Survivors may cling to the loving moments, the apologies, the tenderness, the promises, because they are desperate to believe the relationship can be safe.

Where trauma bonding ties the survivor to fleeting tenderness, cognitive dissonance forces the brain to explain away harm so the two realities can coexist. This absence of recognition is not denial; it is the outcome of systematic grooming and indoctrination.

The perpetrator carefully shapes reality, teaching the survivor to reinterpret harmful behaviours as signs of love. The perpetrator shifts boundaries so gradually that the survivor has learned to see red flags as usual, or even as proof of care, by the time they become visible.

**Carefully designed trap.**

Reward and punishment keep survivors off balance. Affection and kindness appear when they follow the rules, only to be replaced by withdrawal or rage when they do not. Over time, the repetition of the message — "I do this because I love you" — becomes internalised until it feels true. Gaslighting then erodes trust in one's own perceptions, leaving survivors doubting their instincts and memories. Beyond trauma bonds and cognitive dissonance, survivors face a wide range of barriers that reinforce their entrapment.

Abuse gradually erodes self-esteem and convinces survivors they are unworthy of better treatment. Shame grows in the silence, feeding the fear of judgment if they disclose. Survivors hold on to an illusion of control, bargaining with themselves as part of grief: "It can work out. Maybe if I try harder." This bargaining often disguises the hope that love might still redeem the harm. However, love that requires self-erasure is not love it is survival.

Fear of retaliation is constant. Threats to harm survivors, children, pets, or even themselves ensure survivors' compliance. They weigh every decision, accounting for the risk of escalation. Practical barriers compound the fear. Economic dependence, destroyed credit, and lack of access to finances keep survivors trapped. Housing insecurity looms large, with limited refuges, long waitlists, and the risk of homelessness. Threats of custody battles and manipulation of children reinforce dependence, while immigration and visa restrictions add another layer of vulnerability through withheld documents or the fear of deportation. Survivors who depend on the abuser for medication, transport, or daily care face the added risk of losing essential support. High legal costs, limited access to legal aid, and inconsistent responses from courts or police further entrench the cycle.

Social barriers create another layer of isolation. Over time, support networks shrink as friends and family cut off, leaving survivors without a safety net. Cultural and community expectations — the pressure to "keep the family together" — can transform isolation into stigma. Even well-meaning social supports may lack trauma awareness; survivors are told to "just leave" without understanding the fear, shame, and systemic barriers involved. Some faith communities misuse spiritual teachings to reinforce endurance, urging survivors to "pray harder," forgive, or stay because marriage is "for better or worse." What might once have been a source of comfort becomes another instrument of control.

Public perception also plays a role. Abusers often maintain a charming or successful outward image while survivors, exhausted and confused by gaslighting, doubt themselves.

They fear being dismissed as dramatic, unstable, or vindictive. Systemic barriers reinforce these fears: there remains a narrow focus on physical violence, while coercive control and psychological abuse are often overlooked.

Survivors are frequently told, "There is nothing we can do until it happens again."

Child protection systems often cannot recognise patterns of coercive control early. Survivors report feeling judged for "failing to protect" their children rather than supported for attempting to navigate danger. Instead of the source of harm, people frequently hold the survivor responsible. Services that could intervene — such as refuges, counselling, housing, and legal aid — are chronically underfunded. Survivors told there are no beds, or they face months on waitlists, left in limbo. Police responses remain inconsistent; while some officers are trauma-informed and responsive, others minimise the abuse or misidentify the survivor as the aggressor, dismissing coercive control as "just relationship issues." An inconsistent response erodes trust and discourages individuals from seeking help.

The emotional bond remains even after the harm. Trauma bonding and shared history can create paralysing conflict, making survivors feel that leaving equals betrayal. Many come to believe they cannot live without the abuser, who has positioned themselves as indispensable — managing finances, transport, household needs, and daily life. Over time, these roles reinforce dependence and feed the belief that survival outside the relationship is impossible.

While many barriers appear circumstantial — such as money, housing, stigma, and legal systems — they are rarely accidental. Perpetrators deliberately engineer these obstacles as part of coercive control. The goal is not only to dominate in the moment but to make the survivor believe that escape is impossible. Financial sabotage is not about greed; it is about severing independence. Isolation is not about jealousy; it is about dismantling support systems. Threats to take children, destroy reputations, or manipulate legal processes entrap people with calculated strategies.

As Lundy Bancroft observed, abusers foster dependency so that survivors come to believe they cannot survive without the relationship. Over time, that dependency can resemble co-dependency — not because survivors lack strength, but because the abuser's control reshaped their sense of identity. "Who am I without them?" becomes the silent question that keeps many bound. Every time the abuser mocks independence, undermines confidence, or presents themselves as the only one who can meet their partner's needs, the illusion of dependence deepens. Coercive control and co-dependency work hand in hand: one creates reliance, the other sustains the illusion that leaving is impossible.

The question "Why don't they just leave?" overlooks the complex web of psychological, practical, social, and systemic barriers that make leaving both perilous and challenging. Research shows that separation is rarely a single event; it often takes multiple attempts before it becomes permanent — not because of weakness, but because of risk. Naming these barriers matters. It shifts responsibility away from survivors and places it where it belongs: on the abuser, and on the systems that cannot provide adequate safety nets.

## My journey

I cannot even remember how many times I left and returned. Each time I swore it was the last. I was always told they knew me better than I knew myself — that they knew what was best for me. Even when I had orders saying they were not supposed to contact me, they still would, and I did not know how to enforce them. They would tell me to get back into the relationship with threats or promises, telling me they loved me, painting a picture of a future together.

The trap operated exactly as designed, so I went back again, not because I was weak. Part of that trap was co-dependency. I believed I could not live without them. I used to get scared of the most ordinary things: what if I could not mow the lawn? What if my car broke down?

What if something went wrong in the house and I did not know how to fix it?

They had convinced me I did not have the skills to survive on my own, that I needed them for everything. Those thoughts haunted me, and over time, they became a barrier. I did not just feel trapped emotionally; I felt incapable of building a life without them.

I can now see how deliberately they reinforced those fears. Every time they mocked me for not knowing how to do something, every time they reminded me of all the ways I could not cope, it chipped away at my confidence and deepened the co-dependency. What I thought was love or care was control, designed to keep me doubting my ability to stand on my own.

# Identifying Perpetrators and Building Boundaries

Early recognition of unhealthy relationship patterns is not about victim-blaming, but about equipping people with knowledge, language, and confidence to respond when something feels wrong. Understanding how perpetrators groom and manipulate allows survivors to detect red flags sooner, trust their instincts, and take action to protect themselves and those they care about.

Recognising red flags also helps regulate the brain's threat system. When we can identify what is happening, the amygdala settles, and the prefrontal cortex, responsible for clear thinking, can remain active. This chapter builds on the previous one by moving from recognising trauma's impact to proactively safeguarding yourself.

## The Grooming Process

Coercive control rarely starts with overt violence. Instead, it begins with grooming, a gradual shaping of the relationship that gives the perpetrator increasing access, influence, and power. This process is often subtle and seductive, which is why survivors frequently describe feeling swept off their feet before realising what was happening.

## Love Bombing and the Charm Offensive

Many perpetrators begin with intense displays of affection and attention, gifts, compliments, and promises of a shared future. The relationship may move at a whirlwind pace toward exclusivity, living together, or even engagement.

While some whirlwind romances are genuine, love bombing can create a quick emotional attachment, making it harder to notice red flags or slow things down. This tactic can also reappear at the end of a relationship to pull survivors back into the cycle of control.

## The Brain in Early Love

Early romantic attachment releases a surge of dopamine, activating reward centres that make the new partner feel irresistible. As novelty fades, oxytocin and endorphins sustain longer-term bonding. For survivors, these changes in brain chemistry can make red flags harder to recognise and leaving harder to contemplate. The brain rewards closeness, even when danger is present.

## Gradual Isolation

Perpetrators often limit their partner's support networks when they have gained trust by criticising friends or family, showing jealousy, or portraying others as a threat. Over time, survivors find their circle narrowing, not by free choice, but through subtle pressure and guilt.

At first, I thought I was choosing to spend more time with my partner. However, later I realised that someone had gradually discouraged, shamed, or guilt-tripped me, which caused me to step back from friends until I had lost them all.

## Testing Boundaries

Perpetrators often test the waters with minor violations, such as checking phones, making controlling comments, or withdrawing affection when challenged. Each time people tolerate the behaviour, the perpetrators push the boundary further, normalising control. Recognising and responding early is key to stopping escalation.

## Red Flags in Early Relationships

Some early signs of coercive control can be subtle, especially during the dopamine-fuelled excitement of a new relationship. Watch for:

Fast-Tracking Intimacy: Pushing for exclusivity, cohabitation, or marriage within weeks.

Testing Boundaries: Teasing after you have set limits, checking your phone just once.

Jealousy Framed as Love: I love you so much I cannot stand the thought of you with anyone else.

Over-Monitoring Disguised as Care: Demanding constant updates, insisting on shared phone plans or location tracking.

Criticising Friends/Family: Labelling loved ones as toxic for you.

Emotional manipulation: threatening self-harm if you leave, or guilt-tripping you for needing space.

## Evidence-Informed Micro-Boundary Checks (First 3–6 Dates)

**Gentle note:** If you ever feel unsafe while setting a boundary, stop immediately. Your safety is the priority, not the experiment. Step back, seek support, and document what happened if possible.

Micro-boundary checks are small, respectful ways to observe how someone responds to limits early on. They are not tricks, but opportunities to assess whether a potential partner can offer respect, flexibility, and emotional safety before making a deeper investment. Each time you practise, you strengthen your confidence and show your nervous system that healthy relationships honour boundaries.

Examples of Micro-Boundary Checks

Plan-Change Check: Politely change or shorten plans. Healthy partners adjust with ease.

Privacy Check: Decline to share passwords. Healthy partners respect this without question.

Independence Night: Keep plans with friends/family. Healthy partners encourage it.

Pace Check: Say you would like to slow things down. Healthy partners honour your pace.

Mini-Money Boundary: Offer to split the bill. Healthy partners accept without resentment.

Values Disagreement: Share a different opinion. Healthy partners stay curious, not combative.

Compassion Snapshot: Notice how they treat service staff. Respect is consistent, not selective.

Accountability Test: Point out a minor slip-up. Healthy partners apologise and adjust.

Tech Boundaries: Keep Social Media Private at First. Healthy partners respect patience.

Body Autonomy Check: Assert small choices of food, health, or medication. A healthy partner supports autonomy.

## Building Boundaries: Protecting Your Space and Your Safety

Boundaries are not about punishment or control; they are about defining what feels safe and acceptable for you. Respecting your boundaries calms the brain's threat system and allows your prefrontal cortex, the part responsible for clear thinking and decision-making, to remain engaged.

### Key Principles for Building Boundaries

Know Your Limits: Reflect on what makes you feel unsafe or drained, and what you need more of, whether that is time, privacy, or respect.

Communicate Clearly: Use simple I statements. For example: "I'm not comfortable sharing my phone passwords."

Watch the Response: Healthy people accept boundaries. Red flags include anger, sulking, or punishment when you set limits.

Follow Through: A boundary without action is just a wish. Plan how you will respond if someone crosses it.

Strengthen Your Support System: Boundaries are easier to hold when you have trusted allies who remind you that your needs are valid.

Saying no might trigger guilt, especially if someone taught you it is selfish. Remind yourself: protecting your wellbeing is not selfish; it is necessary.

## My journey: Boundaries

For much of my life, I struggled to set boundaries. Someone trained me to please people, always agreeing, over-committing, and neglecting my own needs. Saying no filled me with fear. When I tried, I would over-explain or apologise.

This left me financially, mentally, and emotionally depleted. Having children shifted things: they needed a mum who was not running on empty. Slowly, I realised that protecting my energy was also safeguarding theirs.

It really has been. In the past two years, I have truly stepped into my power. When something threatens my well-being, I can say no without over-explaining or apologising. It can still be difficult, but it is liberating.

As an example, a friend recently asked me to take on a significant volunteer role. In the past, I would have said yes and resented it. This time, I say: "Thank you for thinking of me, but I cannot commit to that right now."

The friend respected my answer, and I felt proud of honouring my needs. Boundaries are a practice, not a onetime event, and each time I set one, I grow stronger.

### Research Insight

Amygdala & Prefrontal Cortex:
When people feel safe, the amygdala (threat detection) reduces activation, allowing the prefrontal cortex to regulate attention, decision-making, and reasoning. Chronic threat or boundary violations dysregulated this balance, shifting behaviour toward

fear-based reactions. Neuroscience has well-documented this. (Arnsten, 2009; McEwen, 2017).
Cortisol & Hippocampal Shrinkage:
Prolonged social stress and isolation can elevate cortisol levels. High sustained cortisol levels are associated with reduced hippocampal volume and impaired memory/learning (McEwen, 2017; Sapolsky, 2015). This supports your claim that survivors may find it harder to trust their judgment or imagine alternatives under coercive control.

Boundaries as a Biological Safeguard:
While "boundaries" are more psychological/social than anatomical, stress regulation research supports the framing: predictable safety signals reduce amygdala overactivation and improve regulatory balance between limbic and cortical systems (van der Kolk, 2014; Herman, 2015). So, describing boundary protection as a biological safeguard is accurate in plain language.

**Reflection Exercise**

Step 1: Spotting Patterns

Think about a relationship (past or present) where you felt drained, unsafe, or small.

What behaviours stood out? Frequent criticism, jealousy, controlling your time, ignoring your "no"?

Ask yourself: Did these behaviours happen once, or were they part of a pattern?

Step 2: Your Internal Signals

Recall how your body responded around that person: Did you feel tense? Did you second-guess yourself? Did you walk on eggshells?

Circle one or two signals that told you something was not right.

Step 3: Boundaries That Protect You

Think about a straightforward boundary you would like to put in place.

Step 4: Looking Forward

Imagine a relationship where someone respects your boundaries.

How would you feel in that space (e.g., calm, safe, valued, free)?

In a relationship, do people already respect your boundaries? Notice how different that feels.

**A gentle note:** Boundaries bring freedom, clarity, and safety, but they also come with loss. Sometimes, setting a boundary means saying goodbye to people who cannot or will not respect your limits. These goodbyes can be painful, even when necessary.

Holding this reality with compassion is essential: you are not too much for wanting respect. Each goodbye makes space for relationships that honour your worth.

Each time you set one, you teach others how to treat you and remind yourself that you are worthy of respect.

# Recognising and Healing Your Attachment Patterns:

Understanding your attachment style is not about putting yourself in a box; it's about uncovering the patterns that shape your relationships. Knowing your style helps explain why some relationships feel magnetic, why you may tolerate unhealthy behaviour, or why leaving can feel impossible.

**Gentle note**: Attachment styles are patterns learned for survival, not character flaws. They are not life sentences. With awareness, safe connection, and practice, they can shift. Your attachment style is an adaptation of the best way your brain knew to keep you safe. That means it is a sign of resilience, not failure. This chapter helps you view your patterns with compassion, rather than shame.

## The Four Main Attachment Styles

### Secure Attachment

What it looks like: comfortable giving and receiving love. Communicates needs clearly without fear of rejection. Balances closeness with independence.

Example:
Two people disagreed about household chores. They each took a moment to calm down, then discussed it further later that night. Neither was worried that the relationship was in danger; they felt safe expressing their needs and working through conflicts.

### Anxious Attachment

What it looks like:

Craves reassurance and fears abandonment. Feels distressed when the other person does not reply quickly. May over-give, "walk on eggshells," or suppress needs to keep the peace. Constant worry about abandonment, even over minor changes. Feeling panicked, restless, or physically sick without reassurance. Relief after contact,

but the cycle quickly starts again.

Example:
A person stares at their phone, heart pounding, checking the time every few minutes. There has been no reply to the text for over an hour.

Their thoughts race:
"Did I do something wrong? Are they upset with me? What if they do not care anymore?"

The anxiety builds until someone sends more messages in a row. "Please just let me know you are safe." "I am sorry if I upset you."

When the reply finally comes, "Just busy, talk later", there is a rush of relief but also shame for "overreacting." Later, the person overcompensates by being overly affectionate and apologetic, hoping to smooth things over and prevent future disconnection.

**Avoidant Attachment**

What it looks like:

Values independence so much that closeness feels threatening. Withdraws during conflict or avoids emotional intimacy. Uses work, hobbies, or busyness to maintain distance.

Example:
One person's partner reached for their hand on the couch and asked, "What is on your mind? You seem distant."

The person inside felt a jolt of panic, as though someone had caught them doing something wrong. Their stomachs clenched, and their first thought was, "I cannot do this right now. I need to be alone."

Instead of answering honestly, they shrugged and said, "I am fine, just tired." They quickly changed the subject to something neutral, like work gossip or TV.

Later that night, they sat in bed scrolling on their phones until their partner fell asleep, feeling secretly guilty for shutting down but also relieved they did not have to talk about their feelings.

## Disorganised / Fearful-Avoidant Attachment

What it looks like: Wants closeness but fears getting hurt, swings between clinging and pushing away. Often linked to childhood trauma or inconsistent caregiving.

Example:
A person may love deeply yet feel constantly on edge. One moment, they send a long message expressing love and devotion; the next, they pick a fight out of nowhere.

Their thoughts are tearing them apart inside. However, if you get too close, you will hurt me. I should push you away before you leave me.

When reassurance comes, they feel calmer, but the relief does not last. A few days later, the cycle repeats. The other person feels exhausted by the emotional whiplash, while the individual secretly blames themselves for not being able to just be normal.

## Can you have more than one style?

Attachment styles exist on a spectrum, and individuals often exhibit traits from more than one style. For example:

You may be secure with friends but anxious in romantic relationships. You might be anxious when someone pulls away, but avoidant when things get too close (common in disorganised attachment). Under stress, even secure people can temporarily become anxious or avoidant. Consistent self-awareness can shift your patterns toward security.

## Neuroscience of Attachment

Attachment is both biological and psychological. Oxytocin, the bonding hormone, enhances communication between the amygdala (which detects threats) and the prefrontal cortex (which regulates emotions). Secure attachment leads to calmer stress responses and improves emotional regulation.

In insecure attachment, these circuits can misfire, leading to hypervigilance or emotional shutdown. Therefore, a secure connection feels calming; it helps your nervous system regulate.

As we have learnt about the hopeful news is that neuroplasticity means your brain can rewire itself. With repeated safe experiences, these circuits can settle, making calm connections easier.

## How Perpetrators Exploit Attachment

Understanding your own attachment style is powerful, but it is equally important to see how others may use those patterns against you, especially in coercive or unsafe relationships.

Anxious love bombing feels intoxicating at first, but withdrawal triggers panic, making compliance more likely.
Avoidant: Guilt trips or emotional pressure exploit the avoidant partner's dislike of conflict.
Disorganised: Hot-and-cold behaviour keeps the victim hooked, swinging between hope and fear.
Secure: Empathy and forgiveness can keep them in unsafe situations longer, leading them to believe that change is possible.

## Protective strategies:

Slow the pace of new relationships. Notice when panic, guilt, or over functioning kicks in. Practise self-soothing (e.g., grounding exercises, breathing techniques). Collaborate with a therapist to build a secure internal base.

## Helpful Strategies for Healing Attachment

Healing after trauma and coercive control often means learning new ways to feel safe, calm, and connected both with yourself and others. These strategies are not about perfection, but about gentle practice. Small steps, repeated often, help rewire the nervous system toward safety and trust.

## My journey

For much of my life, I moved in a cycle of anxious attachment. I craved closeness and constant reassurance, and even the smallest silence could feel like abandonment. I would replay conversations in my mind, scanning for clues that someone might leave or that I was not enough.

That deep hunger for connection often drew me into ignoring red flags, hoping to feel safe — even if only for a moment.

However, when the hurt became overwhelming, when rejection or betrayal cut too deeply, the pendulum would swing hard in the opposite direction. I shut down, withdrew, and built walls around myself for protection. My avoidant side now whispers that I do not need anyone, and I am safer alone, that intimacy can be dangerous. Living between these two extremes — longing and withdrawing — is exhausting, but it was also the only way my nervous system knew to survive.

Healing is still a work in progress. I know my default is to retreat into avoidance. I share this because sometimes people imagine that a therapist, or someone with education and professional titles, must have it all together. We are human too. Our journeys are ongoing, and healing is something we practice, not something we finish.

### Self-Reflection

This is about noticing patterns, not diagnosing.

When I Feel Close (Connection)

Do I relax, or do I feel anxious/overwhelmed?

What body cues show up (ease in chest, tight stomach, restless energy)?

What thoughts appear?

Secure-Ish: "This feels good. I can enjoy it."

Anxious-Ish: "Do not let this go. What if they leave?"

Avoidant-Ish: "This is too much. I need space."

When Someone Pulls Away (Distance/Separation)

Do I pursue, panic, or shut down?

How do I attempt to reconnect (calls/texts, acting "fine," withdrawing)?

What story do I tell myself?

Secure-Ish: "Distance happens; we will reconnect."

Anxious-ish: "It is my fault. I am losing them."

Avoidant-ish: "I knew closeness was not safe. Better on my own."

During Conflict (Activation)

Do I over-apologise, withdraw, or discuss calmly?

What helps me regulate (breathing, time-out, writing it down)?

After Conflict (Repair)

Can I name what hurt and what I need next time?

Do I seek repair, avoid it, or escalate again?

What simple repair script could I try?

When X happened, I felt....... Next time, I can try .....

Do these reactions differ with friends, partners, family, or authority figures?

Where do I feel most secure? What is different there (pace, boundaries, predictability?

# Part Six
# Leaving & Recovery

## Trauma Bonding in Family Violence and Coercive Control

### The Cycle of Abuse and Bonding

Trauma bonding does not just happen. A cycle builds it step by step, and that cycle conditions survivors to stay connected to the person harming them. Psychologist Lenore Walker was one of the first to map this cycle, showing how tension, abuse, reconciliation, and calm form a loop that feeds on itself.

From the inside, the cycle does not always appear obvious. At first, it can feel like ordinary relationship difficulties, like stress, arguments, and apologies. However, slowly, the survivor recognises a rhythm they cannot seem to break. Love and fear become intertwined, hope and despair blur, and leaving feels both unthinkable and unsafe. This is the trap of coercive control: not just physical danger, but emotional conditioning that convinces survivors to stay.

### Tension Building

The survivor feels uneasy, as if something is amiss. They walk on eggshells, monitoring tone, watching body language, and trying to avoid triggers. Anxiety builds as criticism, controlling behaviour, or subtle put-downs accumulate. Survivors refer to this as living in a state of constant readiness. Their nervous systems become hyper-alert, scanning for danger, leaving them exhausted and over-focused on the abuser's moods.

## The Incident

The abuse can appear as yelling, threats, violence, financial control, sexual coercion, or psychological manipulation. Fear, shame, and shock flood the survivor, though rarely surprise, because deep down they have learned to expect it. The body flips into survival mode: fight, flight, freeze, or fawn. Strangely, once the storm breaks, there is a twisted sense of relief that it is over.

## Reconciliation (The "Make-Up" Phase)

After an episode of abuse, the perpetrator often shifts into apology and repair. They may blame stress, alcohol, or even the survivor. Sometimes they show remorse; other times, they minimise what happened. They may also use intense gestures, gifts, affection, or promises of a better future, such as, "I cannot live without you." You are the only one who understands me.

These gestures feel powerful because they arrive unpredictably, right after harm. Survivors cling to them the way a gambler clings to a win, hoping that this time, things will change.

**Is this love bombing?** Sometimes, yes. Love bombing typically refers to the overwhelming affection and intensity that often occurs early in a relationship, aiming to create a rapid attachment.

In the cycle of abuse, the make-up stage can look like love bombing, but it is more about re-securing control after harm. The goal is not genuine repair, but keeping the survivor invested and confused.

## Calm / Honeymoon

For a while, things feel safe. The survivor breathes again, even believes the worst is behind them. This is the next stage of the relationship; it feels new, and Survivors believe they are happy, in love, and loved. Survivors retreat into isolation again, cutting off ties with social connections. People often refer to this phase as reconciliation or working things out, which makes it even harder for survivors to explain what is really happening.

## The Trap of Intermittent Reinforcement

Over time, the survivor learns to endure long stretches of pain for the sake of brief but intoxicating relief. To those outside of a relationship, leaving seems logical. Those inside feel that leaving means abandoning their only comfort, even if that comfort is harmful.

This cycle mirrors addiction. Cruelty combined with kindness can rewire the brain. The rare, tender moments feel disproportionately influential because they come after terror. Every I love you, every apology, every gift becomes a chemical high, a rush of dopamine and oxytocin.

## What is Trauma Bonding?

Trauma bonding is a powerful emotional attachment that forms between a victim and a perpetrator in an abusive relationship. Despite the harm, the bond can feel almost impossible to break. Survivors describe it as the push and pull of cruelty and tenderness, threats and promises, fear and hope.

Dr Patrick Carnes first identified the concept of trauma bonding in the early 1990s. Working with survivors of sexual abuse and addiction, Carnes observed that people often remained intensely attached to those who harmed them. In his book The Betrayal Bond (1997), he defined trauma bonds as dysfunctional attachments that occur in the presence of danger, shame, or exploitation. He claimed that betrayal by someone we depend on can create an even stronger tie than healthy affection.

Later psychologists connected trauma bonding to earlier theories and frameworks:

Cycle of Abuse (Lenore Walker): Walker mapped a repeating pattern of tension, abuse, reconciliation, and calm, a loop survivor often described as "living in a cycle you cannot escape." Relief after each violent episode reinforces attachment to the abuser.

Attachment Theory (John Bowlby): When the same person is both a source of fear and comfort, the need for connection can override the instinct for self-protection. Survivors cling to the abuser because their nervous system perceives the relationship as the only available source of safety.

Neuroscience: Modern brain research shows why the bond feels so powerful. The body releases oxytocin, the bonding hormone, even during abuse, and dopamine spikes during reconciliation phases. These chemical surges intensify the connection and make the relationship feel addictive.

Together, these insights show that trauma bonding is not about weakness or choice; it is the predictable outcome of psychological and biological processes designed for survival but hijacked by abuse.

The following examples illustrate how isolation and coercive control operate, highlighting the devastating impact on both children and adults in long-term domestic violence situations.

### The story of Patty Hearst

People widely recognise the Patty Hearst case as a public example of trauma bonding. In 1974, Hearst, the 19-year-old granddaughter of American media magnate William Randolph Hearst, was kidnapped by the Symbionese Liberation Army (SLA). After weeks of captivity, abuse, and threats to her life, she adopted the ideology of her captors, even taking part in a bank robbery alongside them.

Many judged her as "choosing" the group, but psychologists later explained her behaviour through the lens of Stockholm Syndrome and trauma bonding. Hearst's case illustrated how victims under extreme coercion may identify with or defend their abusers as a means of survival. This behaviour can appear irrational to outsiders, but it makes sense when viewed through the lens of survival science.

### These cannot be real.

These two real-life stories, adapted into Netflix documentaries, illustrate how coercive control operates and the devastating impact it can have on both children and adults.

### Abducted in Plain Sight (2019)

The Broberg family befriends their charming neighbour, "B" (Robert Berchtold), who grooms not only their daughter, Jan, but the entire family.

Manipulation: His most powerful tool was isolation. Through lies, fear, and bizarre "alien abduction" stories, he cut Jan off from her family and controlled her thoughts and actions.

Adults as victims: Berchtold also manipulated the parents, exploiting their trust, shame, and vulnerabilities to stop them from protecting their child.

Key insight: Even intelligent adults are vulnerable to gaslighting and entrapment through coercive control, proving it's not exclusive to children.

Missed intervention: Early recognition of isolation and grooming should have triggered child protection measures. Instead, intervention came only after years of harm.

### The Puppet Master: Hunting the Ultimate Conman (2022)

This series follows Robert Hendy-Freegard, a con artist who convinced multiple adults he was an undercover MI5 agent.

Manipulation: He used fear of imaginary enemies, financial exploitation, and enforced isolation to dominate his victims.

Adults as victims: Men and women gave up careers, families, and money under his control. Sophie Clifton describes rejecting her father through slander while under Robert's influence.

Key insight: The long-term dynamics bore a resemblance to cult-like control, demonstrating that coercive control can entrap even competent adults.

Intervention: Police had to rescue adult victims physically. While the prosecution succeeded, earlier recognition of psychological abuse could have prevented years of harm.

## Psychological Mechanisms

Trauma bonding is not about weakness or choosing to stay. It results from powerful psychological mechanisms that rewire how survivors think, feel, and respond inside an abusive relationship. Two of the most important are cognitive dissonance and the addiction-like pattern of intermittent reinforcement.

## Cognitive Dissonance: The Trauma Bond

Cognitive dissonance and trauma bonding are deeply connected, keeping survivors emotionally bonded. When an abuser insists the violence never happened or calls the survivor crazy for remembering differently, the survivor's mind bends to accommodate that false reality. Over time, trust in their own memory and instincts erodes, making the abuser's reassurances feel like the only ground left to stand on.

## Addiction Parallel

Many survivors describe trauma bonding as feeling like an addiction, and neuroscience backs this up. Mirroring the cycle of dependency is the cycle of abuse:

**The high-** reconciliation after abuse brings apologies, gifts, and affection. The brain releases dopamine (pleasure) and oxytocin (bonding), forming intense relief and closeness.

**The fall** -abuse, neglect, or rejection-comes back. Fear and anxiety flood the body.

**Withdrawal**: When survivors try to leave, panic, insomnia, cravings, and overwhelming loneliness set in. The absence of the high feels unbearable, pulling them back.

This intermittent reinforcement of unpredictable kindness between episodes of harm is the same principle that makes gambling addictive. Survivors never know when the following apology or gift will come, but when it does, the relief is intoxicating.

The chemicals reinforce trauma bonds. Survivors are not choosing to return; their brains and bodies are responding exactly as they would to any addictive pattern. Breaking free requires not just physical safety but the slow rewiring of the nervous system away from dependence on those fleeting highs.

## How Coercive Control Fuels Trauma Bonds

Trauma bonding does not grow in a vacuum. Someone carefully cultivates coercive control, using a web of tactics that blend fear with hope, and cruelty with comfort.

Promises of a better future, such as a holiday, marriage, or counselling, keep hope alive, even when change never comes. Gaslighting tactics twist reality until the survivor doubts themselves, making the abuser's version of events the only truth. Bursts of affection after violence flood the body with relief, resetting the bond.

Abusive partners manipulate not only with intimidation but with manufactured hope, ensuring survivors remain emotionally invested even while being harmed.

### Trauma bonds keep survivors stuck.

They returned after leaving, not because they wanted the abuse, but because the bond felt stronger than logic. Health declines under the stress of constant push-pull. Anxiety, depression, and complex PTSD are common outcomes. Children caught in the middle may confuse control with care, normalising toxic patterns into the next generation. Breaking a trauma bond is not just about leaving. It requires safety, support, and deep healing.

### Breaking the Bond

Recovery often begins with naming the dynamic: this is a trauma bond, not love. That awareness alone can loosen the grip of shame and silence. Understanding the cycle of abuse and trauma bonding helps to reduce self-blame and reframe survivors' actions as survival strategies, not failures.

## Therapeutic Support

Trauma-informed therapies such as EMDR, somatic approaches, and trauma-focused CBT can help survivors process the memories that fuel the bond. These treatments reduce the emotional intensity of trauma triggers and support the nervous system in finding safety again. There are new therapies coming out all the time. A recent one I heard about is ketamine therapy, so watch this space for that.

## Connection and Community

Because isolation deepens the bond, connection is part of breaking it. Group programs and peer support also play a decisive role. I facilitate The Shark Cage® program, developed by Ursula Benstead, a psychologist and clinical supervisor whose work focuses on complex trauma, family and domestic violence, and sexual assault.

The Shark Cage framework employs a metaphor of building protective "bars" or boundaries to keep predators (perpetrators) at a distance, while allowing for safe relational connections — helping survivors resist revictimisation. Practitioner feedback suggests that a shared understanding fosters self-efficacy and reduces feelings of shame and isolation.

## Safety and Independence

Practical support matters as much as emotional healing. Housing, financial counselling, and legal protections help loosen the material ties that keep survivor's dependent. Without these supports, necessity and emotion reinforce trauma bonds.

## Rebuilding Identity

The deepest step is reclaiming a sense of self. Abuse erodes worth and identity; healing can restore them. Narrative and strengths-based approaches help survivors' re-author their stories, moving from 'I stayed' to 'I survived.

## From the Therapy Room: Love, Control, and Glitter in the Healing

Only days after being shoved against a wall and threatened, the perpetrator arrived home with a new car. They handed her the keys and called it proof of love — a sign of commitment, a promise of a shared future. For the survivor, the gesture carried two heavy weights: a fragile hope that change had finally arrived, and a deeper emotional, financial, and symbolic tie to the person who had harmed her.

In the end, they stayed. For them, it felt like the safest or most manageable option. That choice does not mean they condoned the behaviour — it means they did what they needed to survive within the circumstances they faced. Each person's path is unique, and every decision carries its own logic and hope. We all may make choices that feel right for us in that moment, and that too deserves compassion.

My career has provided me with so many memorable moments. I refer to these times as glitter. One of those glimmers comes through facilitating The Shark Cage® program. In these groups, I watch survivors rebuild their sense of safety, self-worth, and power. I have seen voices that once trembled grow steady. I have seen confidence return to eyes that once held only fear.

There are so many proud moments I carry for the people I have had the privilege of walking beside in that space — each one a reminder that healing is possible, that growth can bloom even after devastation. The same control that once confined can, through understanding and connection, become the foundation for freedom.

.

# Safety Planning and Important Things to Consider

Safety planning is about creating choices where coercive control has stripped them away. For survivors, leaving is not a single event but a process that requires preparation, courage, and support.

If you feel overwhelmed by all the possibilities, remember that you do not need to do everything at once. A small step is still a step. Your safety and dignity are priorities.

## Thinking About Support

Identify one or two people whom you feel you can trust and confide in safely. Share a simple code word with them so you can signal danger.

Professional services, including Domestic Violence Services, 1800RESPECT, Legal Aid, and Victims Services, can provide confidential advice and referrals.

Health and well-being: A GP, counsellor, or psychologist can support your mental health, help manage trauma symptoms, and create documentation that may assist in legal processes.

School and childcare staff: inform teachers or administrators of any orders and provide simple instructions on who may collect your children.

Workplace support: Where safe, please notify your employer or HR. Many workplaces have family violence leave entitlements and security protocols.

Community connections: Faith groups, cultural organisations, and community networks can offer emotional or practical support when appropriate.

## Legal Protections

### Family Violence Orders (FVOs)

(Names vary by state/territory in Australia) IVOs—Intervention Orders (VIC)

ADVOs—Apprehended Domestic Violence Orders (NSW) DVOs—Domestic Violence Orders (QLD & NT) ROs—Restraining Orders (WA)

FVOs/PFVOs—Family Violence Orders / Police Family Violence Orders (TAS & ACT)

### What orders may do:

Ban contact, harassment, or stalking.

Restrict access to homes, workplaces, or schools.

Recognise coercive control as a pattern of abuse, not just single incidents.

Provide the police with stronger powers to intervene and act on breaches.

Practical steps: Apply via the police (who can issue urgent interim orders) or at your local Magistrates' Court. Always carry a copy, and provide copies to your child's school, workplace, or trusted friends/family. Request conditions specific to your needs (e.g., safe handover locations for children). Documenting breaches. Prioritise safety all the time. Note dates, times, what people said or did, and any witnesses. Remember, it is about pattern. Screenshots and messages: Save texts, emails, or call logs. Save copies on a secure cloud account or email them to a trusted friend, ensuring you do not lose the evidence if someone takes or wipes your phone. Photos/videos: If safe, capture evidence of damage, stalking, or proximity breaches. Police reports: Report every breach, even if police action feels slow. Each report strengthens the evidence. Inform others: Share this information with schools, childcare providers, neighbours, or employers so they can help notice/report breaches.

### Parenting and Family Law:

Family law can be overwhelming, especially when perpetrators use the system itself for control.

Strategies to consider:

### Seek Advice Early:

Contact Legal Aid, community legal centres, or the Family Relationships Advice Line (1800 050 321) for free advice.

Many lawyers offer initial consultations at no cost.

Parenting Orders:

Consent orders are binding and enforceable by law, unlike informal agreements.

Parenting Plans: Useful for documenting arrangements but not legally enforceable.

Mediation & Family Dispute Resolution:

Compulsory in most parenting disputes under s 60I of the Family Law Act 1975, but not always safe.

Survivors may request a 60I certificate to bypass mediation if there is family violence, child abuse, or risk.

Recovery Orders:

Court orders allow police to locate and return children when a parent withholds them as a control.

Protection Orders & Parenting:

Family Violence Orders (AVOs, IVOs, DVOs): Can include parenting-related conditions (e.g., safe handovers, no contact at school).

These may operate alongside parenting orders; seek legal advice to avoid conflicting conditions.

Supervised Contact & Safety Measures:

Courts can order supervised time where children are at risk.

Handovers can occur at schools or supervised contact centres to minimise direct contact between parents.

Child Protection Involvement:

If the Department of Communities/Child Safety is involved, survivors can request case conferences, safety planning, and legal representation.

Documentation of violence (medical reports, school records, police statements) strengthens cases.

Legal Representation & Support Persons:

Survivors can request to have a support person with them in court.

Specialist Family Violence Units within courts and Legal Aid provide help.

## Financial Safety

Money is one of the strongest levers of control in abusive relationships. Planning small, safe steps toward financial independence can help restore freedom and options.

Strategies to consider:

Paid Domestic Violence Leave (Australia): Each year (as of 2023), employees have the right to 10 days of paid family and domestic violence leave. This leave is separate, and the payslips should not show it to protect confidentiality.

"Fuck Off Fund": A small stash of money (cash hidden safely, or savings in a discreet account) can provide vital independence. Even setting aside $5–$10 regularly builds choice.

Banks and Financial Institutions: Most banks now have dedicated domestic violence support teams that can help survivors open safe accounts, block joint account access, or restructure debt. Inquire about hardship relief, emergency card replacements, or discreet statements sent to a safe address/email.

Centrelink & Victims Services: Centrelink Crisis Payment: Available if you leave because of family violence or are in crisis. Victim Services (state-based): Can provide counselling, safety expenses, and financial help.

Other support: Most states/territories have bond loans or housing grants to assist relocation. Safe Accounts & Access: Open a separate bank account in your name only (using an email/phone number the abuser cannot access). Where possible, change PINs and passwords regularly. Consider using online-only banks for discreet transactions. Debt Protection: Keep copies of financial documents (leases, loans, credit cards, superannuation). Seek legal advice if someone created debts in your name without your consent — you might challenge this financial abuse. Cash Access: Hiding tiny amounts of cash in various safe places (such as a wallet, go-bag, or car) can be beneficial if someone cuts off or tracks cards. If safe, consider exploring flexible work, retraining, or further study options. Most employers offer employee assistance programs (EAPs) that provide free

counselling and support. Unions can also provide advocacy around workplace protections. Community Financial Counsellors: Free, confidential services exist across Australia. They can help with budgeting, debt negotiation, and accessing emergency relief.

## Housing and Safety Options

Safe at Home programs: Allow survivors to remain in their own homes while the order excludes the perpetrator. Support may include security upgrades (such as locks, cameras, and lighting), safety audits, and access to legal and advocacy help. Availability varies by state/territory. Refuges and transitional housing provide short- or medium-term accommodation when remaining at home is not safe. These services may also connect survivors with counselling, financial support, and continuity of children's schooling. Social & community housing: Survivors can apply for priority access to public housing. Even with potentially long wait times, most states prioritise DV cases. Private rental supports include bond loans or rent assistance through state housing departments. Most states allow survivors to break a lease early without penalty if they can show evidence of domestic violence. Utility providers may also waive fees or provide hardship relief in family violence cases.

**Health and Medical Planning**

Preparing in advance ensures continuity of care and reduces risk in crisis moments when health needs may become urgent during separation, especially when accessing medication or treatment.

Medication: Keep a small supply of essential medications stored in a safe but accessible location (e.g., a trusted friend's home, a locked container, or a go-bag). Include children's medications, asthma inhalers, EpiPens, and other urgent prescriptions. Set reminders to rotate supplies so they remain in date. Medical records: ask your GP or health professionals to note disclosures of family violence in your file. This creates an evidence trail if you need legal protection later. Request copies of critical medical records (for you and your children) such as vaccination records, diagnoses, or treatment summaries. Keep these in your go-bag or store them digitally in a password-protected folder. Emergency contacts: Save key contacts (doctor, hospital, supportive friends/family) under neutral names in your phone to avoid raising suspicion. Keep written copies in your wallet or go-bag, in case someone takes or destroys your phone. For children, provide schools or childcare with emergency contact details of safe adults who can pick them up if needed. Health aids and essentials: glasses, hearing aids, mobility devices, and daily health items should be part of your escape kit. If you rely on equipment (e.g., CPAP machines, diabetes supplies), consider preparing a smaller travel version or backup set if possible.

## Mental health supports

Your emergency plan can also include crisis lines, therapists, or counsellors' numbers. Some survivors create a short grounding kit (such as a stress ball, calming scents, a journal, and affirmations) to stabilise themselves during high-stress transitions. Suppose you may need specialist mental health support and services. You can talk to your GP. Sometimes mental health care plans can connect you with a low-fee service that is more than one session.

## Transport & Escape Routes

Having a safe way to leave quickly can make all the difference. Perpetrators often control access to vehicles, keys, or money to limit options, so preparing transport in advance helps restore choice and safety. Spare keys: Keep a spare set of car keys hidden somewhere the abuser cannot access (with a trusted friend, at work, or in a secure place outside the home). Fuel: Always try to keep your vehicle at least half full of fuel. A full tank can provide the freedom to leave with no need to stop. Public transport access: Carry a charged public transport card or keep change for buses/trains. Know the nearest stops and timetables. Ride-share or taxi: Download and set up accounts for ride-share apps (Uber, Ola, Didi) in advance and, if possible, keep a small amount of cash or a prepaid card for emergencies.

Safe driver contacts: Identify trusted people who can pick you up at short notice. Have their numbers memorised as well as saved. Parking strategy: If possible, park your car facing the road for a quicker exit. Avoid being blocked in by other vehicles. Back-up routes: Know more than one way out of your neighbourhood — perpetrators sometimes track or intercept routine routes.

Accessibility needs: If you rely on mobility aids or public services, ensure you have backup arrangements (e.g. wheelchair-accessible taxi numbers or local disability transport services).

## Pets

Safe-care programs: Services like RSPCA Safe Beds for Pets, Pets in Crisis, and state-based DV pet fostering programs can offer temporary housing until survivors settle. Planning: If safe, prepare a small bag with pet food, medication, and favourite toys/blankets to reduce stress for the animal. Vet records: keep copies of vaccination and microchip details in your emergency documents. This helps you reclaim your pet and prove ownership if someone challenges it. In Australian states, there is a movement toward including animals under domestic violence/protection orders. In New South Wales (NSW), reforms now classify harming or threatening to harm animals as intimidation in domestic violence cases. Police acknowledge that threatening an animal can be a means of intimidation or coercion.

## Possessions

Prioritise essentials: focus first on documents, medications, keys, devices, and children's items. You can usually replace clothes and household goods. I know often things have sentimental value, yet you are more valuable!

The national leaving violence program helps with the costs of leaving. Victim Services: State-based services may provide financial support to replace furniture, appliances, or personal items lost through violence or fleeing. Safe storage: if possible, leave a packed bag with a trusted friend or family member. Some refuges also offer storage options. Bring old phones, USB drives, or laptops containing evidence or contacts. Forensic experts can sometimes access them even if broken.

## Safeguarding Documents & Evidence

Critical documents: Keep copies of passports, birth certificates, Medicare cards, driver's licences, bank cards, and legal orders such as custody orders and FVOs. Store originals if safe, and digital copies on a secure cloud or with a trusted contact. Evidence of abuse: save texts, emails, and voicemails. Journal incidents with dates, times, and witnesses. Photograph injuries, damaged property, or stalking behaviours.

Email evidence to a new account with a secure password. Use a hidden or encrypted app to store files if it's safe to do so. Give a copy to a lawyer, counsellor, or trusted friend so you do not carry all the risk. Patterns matter: Courts and services often act on a pattern, not one-off events. Keeping a timeline helps show escalation.

## System Abuse

Perpetrators often extend coercive control into the courtroom, a tactic sometimes called legal abuse or paper abuse. Instead of physical violence, the system itself becomes the weapon. Survivors may experience:

Repeated Applications: Endless filings to drain time, money, and emotional energy.

Cross-Examination: Attempts to intimidate survivors directly in court (now limited under the Family Law Act but still occurring in some matters). Delay Tactics: Drawing out proceedings so survivors remain in limbo, financially and emotionally.

Misusing allegations or making fake and malicious allegations. Withholding Children: Ignoring orders or engineering disputes to force ongoing contact. Survivors can apply for orders preventing direct cross-examination (legal representation required instead). Document everything: keep copies of emails, texts, and applications to show patterns of misuse. Safety planning in court: Survivors can request separate waiting areas, staggered entry/exit, or remote testimony via video link. System abuse reinforces the reality that leaving an abuser is not always the end of the abuse. Survivors need both legal remedies and systemic reform to ensure their safety. Naming this pattern helps remove the shame associated with it, placing accountability on those who exploit the legal process to maintain power.

## Gentle Note About Personal Safety

Before moving into safety planning, please take a moment to check in with yourself. Reading about coercive control, barriers, and survival strategies can bring up powerful emotions and memories. If you are feeling overwhelmed, it is okay to pause, step away, or talk to someone you trust.

Safety planning is robust, but it can also stir up feelings of fear or urgency. Remember, you do not have to do everything at once. Small steps are still steps forward. Your safety, physical and emotional well-being come first. If you feel unsafe right now, please reach out to local emergency services or a trusted support organisation.

Take a deep breath, centre yourself, and know this: you are not alone.

### Self-Reflection: Your Safety Plan

1. What Makes You Feel Safe?

What do you need right now to feel safer in daily life?

Are there priorities you need to balance with safety (e.g., work, school, children's needs)?

What are your warning signs that things may escalate? (tone, words, behaviour you have seen before).

2. Looking Back

What have you tried in the past to keep safe?

What worked?

What did not feel helpful?

How might an abuser react if they suspect you are planning to leave or seek support?

3. Relationship Choices

Do you want to remain in the relationship?

If not, do you want or need to remain in contact with the person (for parenting, work, or other reasons)?

4. Support Networks

Do you have one or two people you feel you can trust and confide in?

Could you share a code word or signal with them to alert them if you are in danger?

Do you have access to professional support (DV services, counsellors, helplines, Legal Aid, Victims Services)?

If you have children, do they know a safety protocol (e.g., where to go, who to call)?

5. Home and Living Arrangements

Do you currently share a home with the perpetrator?

Does the perpetrator have access to your home, even if you live in a separate location?

Do you know which rooms are safest (easy exits, fewer weapons) and which to avoid (kitchen, bathroom, garage)?

If you needed to escape, which exits would you use?

6. Practical Safety Questions

Could you use transport to get to a safe place (car, public transport card, ride-share)?

If you need to leave suddenly, can you access money?

Can you stay somewhere safe (friend, family, refuge, housing)?

Would you feel comfortable calling the police in an emergency?

Do you have pets?

Do you need to vary your routines (routes to work, school, shopping) to avoid predictability?

## 7. Securing Essentials

Is a safe phone available to you (one that is unmonitored/untracked)?

Do you need to secure or change passwords for accounts?

Are you keeping safe copies of important documents, such as IDs, passports, and birth certificates?

Do you keep essential medication in a safe place?

Do you have a go bag ready (clothes, charger, documents, cash, children's items)?

## 8. Technology and Evidence

Have you checked for spyware or unusual apps on your devices?

Have you disabled location-sharing features?

Do you need a new phone, SIM card, or email for sensitive matters?

Are you keeping screenshots of abusive messages or financial evidence (if safe to do so)?

Do you document incidents (dates, times, photos of damage or injuries)?

9. After Leaving / Transition Safety

Do you need to change locks or improve home security (locks, cameras, alarms)?

Do you need to notify your workplace, school, or childcare provider about your situation and provide them with copies of the court orders?

Have you connected with banks, Centrelink, or Victims Services for financial and practical support?

Do you know how to report breaches of family violence orders or parenting orders?

Final Reflection

What is one small step you could take this week to increase your safety?

Who can you reach out to for support at this time?

What words of encouragement would you give yourself as you move forward?

# Recovery & Resilience— Healing After Coercive Control

Recovery after coercive control is not quick, and it is not simple. The moment someone reaches safety, the patterns of fear, shame, and self-doubt do not vanish. Survivors describe feeling lost.

The human body and mind can both survive adversity and repair themselves. Even in families that have endured years of coercion and conflict, moments of joy, laughter, and peace can still return. Healing is not about erasing the past; it is about learning what you truly want in your future.

For children, recovery often begins the moment they experience consistent safety. For adults, it may come through grief, trauma work, self-discovery, and the slow rebuilding of trust. Both journeys matter. Both take time; both remind us that surviving was never the end of the story; healing is.

## The Science of Healing

Researchers once believed that the effects of childhood trauma and toxic stress were permanent. We now know this is not true. Science tells us that our brains and bodies are adaptable. The same neuroplasticity that allowed survival in a coercive environment also allows repair once safety is restored.

Neuroplasticity: the brain can rewire itself across the lifespan. In safe environments, neural pathways shaped by fear can gradually weaken, while new pathways associated with calmness, learning, and joy become stronger.

Under coercive control, the stress response (the HPA axis) becomes over-activated, releasing cortisol in constant cycles that affect sleep, digestion, mood, and memory.

When safety returns, cortisol levels stabilise. Over time, the body can relearn how to distinguish between danger and safety.

Case studies and clinical work reveal that children who were once anxious, withdrawn, or aggressive often thrive again in safety, stability, and support. Adults, too, describe post-traumatic growth, discovering resilience, creativity, and compassion that they did not know they possessed while entrapped.

Healing does not mean going back to who you were before. It means growing into someone who carries their scars with strength. They can teach their children that love does not have to hurt, learning that safety and peace are not only possible but deserved.

### Children's Recovery Pathways

Children living with coercive control are often hypervigilant, anxious, or withdrawn. However, a safe, stable, and nurturing environment can help children change rapidly and profoundly.

Safety as Foundation: Research shows that children's stress systems regulate within weeks of being removed from violent or coercive homes. Sleep improves, nightmares decrease, and physical symptoms, such as stomach-aches, often resolve.

Stable Routines: Consistency is healing. Predictable meals, regular school attendance, and consistent bedtime rituals signal to a child's nervous system that the world is safe.

Secure attachments: Children can rebuild trust when caregivers respond with patience, calmness, and reliability. Even if damaged, people can restore trust over time and with consistency.

### Healing with a child

A nine-year-old who once flinched at every loud noise began laughing freely again after six months in a safe home. Their teacher reported a remarkable change: from withdrawn and failing at school to curious and engaged. The change was not magic; it was safety, stability, and connection.

Children's recovery is not about forgetting what happened. It is about discovering that love can feel safe, and that their world does not have to be ruled by fear.

### Adult Recovery & Post-Traumatic Growth

For adults, recovery is more complicated. Survivors often carry shame and grief: shame for staying, shame for what the children saw, grief for the years lost. Healing involves facing these wounds with compassion rather than blame.

Moving from Survival Mode to Self-Discovery: After years of hypervigilance, the nervous system may resist calm. Survivors sometimes describe feeling restless or unsafe in what should be a peaceful setting. Learning to sit with safety takes practice.

Rebuilding Trust: Coercive control shatters trust — in others, in systems, and in oneself. Recovery means slowly learning to trust again, starting with small, safe relationships.

Stages of Growth: Survivors describe experiencing stages, including anger, grief, disorientation, and ultimately, a sense of growth. Not everyone follows the same path, but the common thread is rediscovering the strength that once felt out of reach.

**I realised that surviving had made me strong in ways I had not seen. My strength is different now; it is not about enduring pain but about choosing peace.**

**Post-traumatic growth does not erase the harm. However, it can also bring meaning, compassion, and resilience that survivors use to rebuild their lives and break cycles for the next generation.**

**-Survivor.**

## Supports That Help Recovery

Recovery is not a solitary process. Survivors and children heal best with support that recognises trauma and meets them where they are.

Therapy Approaches: EMDR, somatic therapy, trauma-focused CBT, and art therapy all help reprocess trauma. Importantly, therapists must tailor therapy because no single method works for everyone.

Community & Peer Support: Isolation feeds shame. Connection, whether through support groups, online communities, or friendships, helps survivors feel less alone.

Joy & Play as Resistance: Simple practices — such as dancing, gardening, painting, and playing with children — become radical acts of repair. They remind survivors that life is not only about surviving but about living.

## Building Resilience Together

Recovery is most potent when shared between a parent and a child. Survivors often describe healing alongside their children, each learning new ways of relating.

Co-Healing: When parents model calm, apologise for mistakes, and show unconditional love, children learn that safety is possible.

Recovery can also include your pets... mine are just so precious.

Everyday Practices: cooking together, planting a garden, or creating family rituals help children rebuild trust and belonging.

Breaking Cycles: By showing children that love is not control, survivors disrupt intergenerational trauma and offer new templates for healthy relationships.

**"I started by planting a garden with my kids. We would water the plants each day, and little by little, they grew. It gave us hope that something beautiful could grow in our lives, too."     - Survivor.**

### Research Insight

Studies also show that if children leave coercive environments, their stress systems can recalibrate. Over time, this may support better sleep, stronger immune function, and improved learning outcomes (McEwen, 2017; ANU, 2023).

Post-traumatic growth: Survivors of trauma, including family violence, sometimes describe unexpected forms of growth in the aftermath. Studies of post-traumatic growth highlight themes of personal strength, deeper relationships, and a greater appreciation for life (Tedeschi & Calhoun, 2004).

Systems and healing: The Australian Law Reform Commission has emphasised that fragmented legal and service systems make recovery more complex for families affected by violence (ALRC Report 114). Trauma-informed research further underscores that safety and stability are the most critical foundations for healing (Herman, 2015; van der Kolk, 2014

**Gentle Note**: Healing is not a linear process. There will be setbacks, flashbacks, arguments, and old triggers. This does not mean failure. Every minor act of safety, kindness, and love is part of recovery.

You are rebuilding. Every day you choose peace; you are teaching your children and yourself that life can be different.

# Becoming You: The Work of Self-Discovery and Self-Care

One of the most insidious effects of coercive control and trauma is the erosion of identity. Over time, you may stop recognising yourself outside the roles imposed on you: caretaker, peacekeeper, partner, parent, or even survivor. The constant demands of abuse and the survival strategies you have had to adopt can make you lose touch with who you are.

When someone else has shaped your life, questioning 'Who am I?' can feel overwhelming or even frightening. However, rediscovering yourself is one of the most critical steps in reclaiming freedom. You are more than what happened to you.

 Here is where self-care and self-love play a crucial role. For survivors, the idea of putting their own needs first can feel almost impossible. Years of coercive control, abuse, or neglect teach you that your value lies in serving others, keeping the peace, or staying invisible. Self-care can feel selfish, and self-love can feel dangerous.

That is why choosing to care for yourself is not just an act of kindness; it is an act of courage. Rediscovering your identity and learning to love yourself are not luxuries; they are essential parts of becoming yourself again.

People misunderstand self-care as indulging in things like bubble baths, candles, or treating yourself. While those things can bring comfort, authentic self-care after trauma is deeper. It is about tending to your body, mind, and spirit in ways that rebuild safety and balance. It is about giving yourself permission to have needs and then meeting them with consistency and compassion.

When your nervous system has been on high alert for years, what you eat, how you rest, how you move, and the boundaries you set to become a solid foundation.

## How Coercive Control Erodes Selfhood

Coercive control affects not only the body but also the mind and spirit. Over time, the constant criticism, gaslighting, and manipulation erode a person's sense of self. Survivors often describe feeling like shells of their former selves, disconnected from their own opinions, dreams, and values. Identity becomes shaped by their survival: What will keep them calm? Rather than what do I want?" Saying no makes boundaries feel unsafe, and as a result, the self becomes secondary to the perpetrator's demands. Someone might scrutinize or control even your small preferences, like the music you like, your style of dress, and how you spend your money. Survivors no longer trust their own choices, especially if they were never taught about choice, or even know that they can have choices.

## Signs You May Have Lost Touch with Yourself

It is hard to notice when you have drifted away from your core identity.

Signs include:

You find it hard to make even small decisions without orders or direction.

You apologise excessively, even when you have done nothing wrong.

You have lost touch with your genuine hobbies, foods, and activities.

Your body feels disconnected; you go along with things you do not want because saying no feels unsafe.

You feel guilty for resting, setting boundaries, or prioritising yourself.

You use others' emotions as a compass: If they are okay, then I must be okay.

If these feel familiar, it does not mean you have failed. It means you have adapted to survive. Adaptation is a sign of resilience, not weakness.

## Self-Reflection: Your Values Identification

Survivors often describe feeling like their choices, dreams, and priorities no longer belong to them, but to the person who controlled them. Healing involves slowly reclaiming those lost parts and reconnecting with the values that guide you as an individual.

Why do Values Matter?

Psychological research shows that living in alignment with your personal values, rather than being driven by fear or obligation, is associated with greater well-being and resilience. Values are not goals you achieve; they are the compass points, what you stand for, that guide your direction in life.

Take a quiet moment to reflect on the following prompts. Journal your answers, discuss them with a therapist, or pause and notice what feels true for you.

Identity

When I think about who I am, what words or roles feel vital to me?

What parts of myself feel silenced or diminished right now?

### Relationships

In the relationships I value, how do I want to show up (e.g., with kindness, honesty, patience)?

What do I need from others in return?

### Parenting or Caregiving (if relevant)

What qualities do I most want to model for my children or those I care for?

What kind of family culture do I want to create?

### Personal Growth

What activities make me feel most like myself?

When have I felt proud, fulfilled, or at peace?

### Boundaries

Self: Which values are non-negotiable for me (e.g., respect, safety, trust)?

How can I protect these values when making choices?

## Back to Basics: Reclaiming the Foundations of Wellbeing

Healing from trauma is not only about therapy or insight; it is also about rebuilding the everyday foundations that keep the body and mind steady. Survivors often describe feeling disconnected from their basic needs, as if survival has pushed nourishment, rest, and movement to the background. Re-establishing these practices is not indulgence; it is repair.

## Nutrition and Gut Health

Eating balanced meals is more than physical fuel; it is a foundation for emotional stability. When blood sugar drops, it can mimic or worse anxiety, causing irritability, mood swings, and difficulty concentrating. Regular meals that include protein, complex carbohydrates, and healthy fats help stabilise energy and reduce these swings.

Emerging research in nutritional psychiatry highlights how the gut–brain axis shapes mood. The gut hosts trillions of microbes that produce neurotransmitters, such as serotonin and dopamine, which play a central role in emotional regulation. In fact, the gut makes up to 90% of the serotonin.

For survivors, chronic stress can disrupt the gut lining, leading to a leaky gut, reduce microbiome diversity, and increase inflammation. Prioritising whole, nourishing foods is therefore not just self-care; it is an active support for brain repair and emotional recovery.

## Why Sleep Matters for Healing?

Sleep is not a luxury; it is a necessity for survival. Poor sleep also increases the amygdala's activity, which worsens anxiety, irritability, and reactivity. Trauma survivors often experience elevated cortisol at night, disrupting circadian rhythms. Restoring these rhythms lowers stress load and restores balance.

Practical strategies for better sleep: Consistent bedtime routines signal safety to the nervous system. Limit screens 30–60 minutes before bed to protect melatonin release. Weighted blankets, soft lighting, or grounding objects can help reinforce feelings of safety. It is also advisable to cut back on caffeine and alcohol, especially at night. Gentle mind-body tools (breathwork, relaxation, meditation) help shift from fight-or-flight to rest-and-digest. Be patient; even one extra hour of sleep per night can reduce depression and anxiety symptoms.

## Movement and the Brain

Trauma often leaves the body in a state of "fight, flight, or freeze," storing stress in the muscles and keeping the nervous system hyper-alert. Movement helps discharge this energy and signals to the body that safety is possible.

## Why movement matters neurochemically:

Endorphins: natural painkillers and mood boosters.

Dopamine restores motivation and reward pathways.

Serotonin plays a crucial role in supporting mood, sleep, and appetite.

BDNF (Brain-Derived Neurotrophic Factor): promotes the growth of new brain cells and connections, particularly in the hippocampus. Cortisol regulation lowers baseline stress hormones.

Gentle, enjoyable movement — walking, yoga, swimming, and dancing are enough to rebuild the body's sense of calm and vitality.

My dogs are my motivators.

## Rest and the Healing Nervous System

Proper rest is more than sleep. For survivors whose bodies trained themselves to stay alert, rest can feel unsafe or foreign. However, intentional pauses are essential for resetting the stress response.

The science of rest: Activates the parasympathetic system, lowering cortisol and heart rate. Shrinks the amygdala and strengthens the prefrontal cortex. Activates the default mode network (DMN), which supports reflection, meaning making, and identity repair. Strengthens immunity and lowers inflammation.

Practical ways to rest:

Short mindfulness or body-scan meditations. Journaling or tea rituals provide structured pauses. Nature-based rest: sitting outside, noticing sound and smell.

Lying down with music or silence. Whatever works for you!

**Gentle note**: Rest is not laziness. It is recovery. Survivors often need to reclaim rest as a right, not a reward.

## Kindness With Boundaries

Self-love also means protecting your energy. For survivors, boundaries feel frightening because they risk conflict or abandonment. However, boundaries are acts of kindness — to yourself and to others.

Brené Brown (2010) describes boundaries as the foundation of compassion: only when we are clear about what we can and cannot give, can we offer love without resentment? Boundaries remind us: I am worthy of respect. I can care for others without abandoning myself.

Examples include saying, 'I need time to think about that,' before agreeing, and turning off your phone at night. Declining invitations that drain energy. Ending conversations when they become unsafe.

**Boundaries are not walls. They are doors, and you decide when they open.**

**-Survivor**

## What Fills Your Cup?

There is a simple but powerful analogy often used in trauma recovery: you cannot pour from an empty cup. Survivors of coercive control usually spend years pouring into other partners, children, and workplaces until their own cup runs dry. Relearning how to refill your cup is not indulgent; it is a matter of survival.

### The Cup Analogy

Imagine your emotional or mental capacity as a cup.

Everyone's cup is a different size, shaped by genetics, trauma, stress, and support systems.

Throughout the day, stress, demands, and sensory input fill the cup — arguments, loud noise, pain, deadlines, worries, etc.

When the cup overflows, it represents a meltdown, shutdown, or emotional overwhelm because your nervous system has reached its limit.

## The Spoon Theory

Every task or interaction costs a certain number of spoons.

Waking up, showering, working, cooking — each uses one or more.

When you're out of spoons, you're done; you can't borrow from tomorrow without consequences (fatigue, burnout, emotional crash).

## The Battery Charger Metaphor

Think of yourself as a battery-powered system:

Your battery drains from stress, sensory load, emotional labour, or unsafe environments.

Rest, connection, therapy, faith, creativity, or nature act like a charger.

But if the "charging cable" (self-care or supportive people) breaks or becomes intermittent, you never fully recharge — so you're constantly operating on low power.

The "drain" might be ongoing hypervigilance or trying to keep others safe.

The "charger" might be moments of genuine rest, connection, or kindness that refill energy reserves.

Everyone has a cup, a spoon, or a battery that holds their emotional energy. When too much stress fills the cup, uses up too many spoons, or drains the battery, we can't function or connect proper.

Learning to recognise what fills your cup and what drains it is an act of self-awareness and self-compassion. The things that refill your cup might be moments of calm, connection, creativity, or rest. The things that drain it may be stress, toxic relationships, or environments that don't feel safe. By noticing these patterns, you can set boundaries and build a life that nurtures your energy rather than depletes it.

## From the Therapy Room: Discovering Your Love Language

One practical tool I often share is the concept of love languages. Many individuals and couples are unaware that people express and receive love in different ways, and that mismatches can cause unnecessary hurt or misunderstanding.

The five primary love languages are:

Words of Affirmation: feeling valued through kind, encouraging, or appreciative words.

Acts of Service: showing love through helpful actions.

Receiving gifts involves thoughtful tokens or gestures that show someone remembered you.

Quality Time: undivided attention and presence.

Physical Touch: comfort and connection through touch, such as hugs or holding hands.

You may have more than one, and they can shift. Identifying your love language helps you understand what makes you feel truly seen and cared for — not only in romantic relationships, but in friendships, family, and even in how you practise self-love. A simple way to discover yours is to notice: What am I not getting? What do I appreciate most when someone offers it? Online quizzes and Chapman's book The Five Love Languages can also be helpful starting points.

## My journey: sugar, ADHD, and self-care

For a long time, I had what felt like an uncontrollable addiction to sugar. I would wake up in the morning and Immediately stuff marshmallows into my mouth, chasing what I now recognise as a quick dopamine hit. My victim's counsellor gently suggested that I might consider being assessed for ADHD. It was not something I had ever imagined applied to me.

As part of my self-care journey, I underwent testing, and the results confirmed what I had not expected — I do, in fact, have ADHD. Understanding this brought so much clarity. It helped me make sense of why I struggled with certain parts of daily life and how my symptoms overlapped with PTSD.

One of the most complicated steps was accepting medication as scaffolding. I had always resisted the idea of relying on tablets; I thought it meant weakness. Over time, I came to realise that medication could be a tool — not something that defined me, but something that supported me. Medication is only one slice of a pizza for my treatment

For me, self-care is not about denial or pride. It is about recognising my needs and choosing the tools that help me thrive.

Stillness has never come naturally to me. A friend once laughed and called it my *"rabbit hopping"* — the way I move from one thing to another to avoid sitting still and processing. It has taken considerable effort to learn to slow down, and even now, I believe I will always be someone who finds peace through action. My version of rest does not always look like stillness it looks like prayer, meditation, and quiet moments where my mind can finally settle.

Sleep has been another challenge. For years, nightmares and flashbacks kept me from feeling safe enough to rest truly. Even now, I often fall asleep with the TV playing softly in the background, the sound acting as a kind of safety blanket. Recently, I have used sleep-frequency videos on YouTube — the ones that promise, *"You will be asleep in five minutes."* I have not found one that delivers yet, but the search itself has become a minor act of hope, a reminder that I am still learning, still healing, and still trying.

# Voice without a choice

This chapter does not blame anyone who chooses silence. Speaking out is a deeply personal act, and for some, it may not feel safe, possible, or even correct. Choosing silence is not weakness. It is a matter of survival, and survival is a powerful force.

I never set out to be in the public eye. I am not someone who enjoys the spotlight or chases recognition. I have always seen myself as a quiet achiever, someone who works hard behind the scenes, wary of big egos and the noise that often comes with public platforms.

When my photo and story appeared on the front page of a newspaper without my knowledge, I felt mortified. It clashed with my instinct to remain small and unnoticed, making me feel exposed.

However, at that moment, I realised something important. If I genuinely wanted to be effective, to challenge coercive control, to advocate for survivors, to change systems, then I would need to raise my professional profile. I didn't want to raise my profile for vanity or recognition; I wanted to be well-known enough to be involved in important decision-making. Advocacy requires visibility. For me, stepping into that uncomfortable space is not about ego; it is about purpose.

Throughout history, progress has always come from those who refused to accept injustice as "normal." Laws have changed, systems have shifted, and awareness has grown only because ordinary people stood up and demanded something better. The same is true of coercive control today. For too long, people have hidden, minimised, or misunderstood it. Change requires persistence, courage, and the willingness to speak, even when your voice shakes.

I was told to cease selling my first book or face court orders and the risk of possible criminal convictions. That was a hard decision. I had to think carefully and strategically, because criminal charges would have undermined the bigger purpose for which I was fighting.

This was supposed to be the book they warned her not to write, but now it has developed into something different. It is no longer about telling my story; it is about offering a resource — a guide to recognising coercive control and a call for change.

I have stood before police officers in academies and meeting rooms; I shared my story and professional insights so they could understand the patterns of family violence and coercive control beyond just isolated incidents. Their letter of thanks was not about me; it was about recognising that lived experience is a teacher.

I have attended many public speaking events to raise awareness, supported community projects, taken part in advocacy, and responded to media requests. Most recently, I have been developing education packs that use true-life examples and documentaries to help people recognise the patterns of coercive control in ways that connect with their own learning style.

Currently, I am on a personal mission to write to various members of parliament, pushing for change in family courts and child protection systems. This will better protect children who are experiencing significant emotional abuse through coercive control.

My next goal is to address the statute of limitations in the reporting of coercive control. Currently, Tasmania has a 12-month statute. Trauma does not work to a deadline. Survivors deserve time to find their voices, not punishment. Reforming this law is not just a matter of legal housekeeping; it is an act of justice.

## What Can You Do If Advocacy Calls to You?

**Gentle Note:** Advocacy is powerful, but it can also be exposing. Speaking out may bring healing, but it can also bring challenges, re-triggering trauma, straining relationships, or inviting backlash from those who do not want change.

It is important to remember. You do not owe your story to anyone. Sharing is a choice, not a requirement. Think about privacy. Once you make something public, you cannot retract it. Consider your legal and professional context, especially if systems or people are still involved in your life.

Advocacy is most effective when grounded in safety and security. Ensure you have support from trusted individuals, services, or professionals to lean on.

A submission written anonymously, a conversation with a decision-maker, or a gentle educational moment in your community — all advocacy counts.

Whilst I may seem to contradict myself by saying I have to raise my profile, that is simply the position that developed and morphed over time from the hidden advocate to the visible one.

Not everyone will feel called to activism, and that is okay.

If you felt the pull toward advocacy, there are ways to start that do not require standing on a stage or being featured on the front page of a newspaper. Advocacy can be quiet, steady, and deeply personal. You can share your story safely by using a blog, artwork, or a trusted community project anonymously or pseudonymously. Storytelling, even in small ways, can break the silence and create a connection.

Support local initiatives, volunteer for a community service, contribute to awareness events, or help with behind-the-scenes tasks that keep advocacy projects running. Write letters or submissions: A single letter to a member of parliament on any level adds to a chorus of voices; policy nudges matter. Use creative expression: art, poetry, or music can communicate truths that statistics cannot. Survivors often find these forms both healing and powerful for advocacy. Join survivor or peer groups: Collective voices carry weight. Groups offer support, safety in numbers, and a platform for shared action. Educate within your circle: Share resources or documentaries with friends, colleagues, or at your school. Small ripples of awareness often spread further than you think. Advocate for children: speak up for trauma-informed practices in schools, childcare, or youth programs. Sometimes advocacy is at the kitchen table or the school gate.

Model boundaries and healing: Living your truth, setting boundaries, and showing resilience are, in themselves, forms of advocacy. Survivors watching may feel less alone, and perpetrators learn that silence no longer protects them.

I began my advocacy journey reactively, through my first writing. It was deeply personal and a way of clearing out the closet of experiences that had weighed heavily on me for years. Writing it was cathartic but also confronting.

While the book used de-identified characters, I now reflect that my children's lives and identities are deeply their own, and not mine to narrate. Parts of that first book were raw and personal; today, I carry a stronger awareness of how public storytelling can ripple outward to those connected to me. That awareness shapes how I write and advocate now.

Speaking out can be powerful, but it also has consequences for ourselves, for our children, and for those connected to us. I do not share this to discourage advocacy, but to invite care: consider timing, privacy, and the next generation that may inherit what you share.

# Part Seven
# A Different Future

## Frequently Asked Questions: Supporting Someone Experiencing Abuse

People often ask all kinds of questions when they suspect coercive control or abuse, so I added this Q&A with the most common things asked. The goal is to provide clear, compassionate answers that keep both survivors and supporters safe.

Q: Would couples counselling work if there is domestic violence or coercive control?
A: Most times, no. Therapists do not recommend couples counselling when abuse is present. That is because. Abuse is about power and control, not communication issues. Sessions can put the survivor at greater risk if the abusive partner retaliates afterwards. Counselling assumes both partners are equally responsible, but only the abusive partner is accountable for their behaviour.

Safer Alternatives:

Individual counselling for survivors to build safety and recovery.

Behaviour-change programs for the person using abuse (not just anger management).

Specialist family violence services for support and safety planning.

Couples counselling may only be safe after abuse has ended, the abusive partner has taken responsibility through a proper program, and the survivor feels genuinely safe and even then, only with a counsellor trained in domestic and family violence.

Q: How do I identify coercive control behaviours?
A: Look for patterns rather than one-off incidents. Is your friend's partner isolating them from others, constantly checking their phone, controlling money, or criticising them in public? These behaviours often add up to a bigger picture of control, even if they do not look extreme on their own.

Q: If I see concerning behaviour, what should I do?
A: First, check your own safety. If it is safe, you can gently let your friend know what you have noticed without judgment, for example, "I have noticed you seem anxious when they call you. Are you okay?" Offer support rather than advice.

Q: Should I speak to my friend directly?
A: Yes, but only if it feels safe. Choose a private moment where the abuser cannot overhear. Respect that your friend may not be ready to talk. Letting them know you are there for them plants a seed of support.

Q: As a witness, how do I safeguard myself?
A: Witnessing abuse can be distressing. It is okay to seek support for yourself, whether from a counsellor,

a helpline, or a trusted person. Protect your boundaries; you cannot "fix" the situation alone.

Q: Should I keep documentation of what I see and hear?
A: Yes, if safe to do so. Notes about dates, times, and what you observed may be helpful if your friend later seeks legal protection. Keep them secure and never share them with the abuser.

Q: When is the right time to approach the person I am worried about?
A: There is rarely a perfect time. Look for small windows of safety when they are alone, calm, and not under immediate stress. Even if they push you away, knowing you care can help them feel less isolated.

Q: What advice can I safely give?
A: Avoid telling them to "just leave." Instead, focus on validating their feelings and offering options: "There are services that can help if you want me to share them." Let them set the pace.

Q: Should I encourage a safety plan?
A: You can ask gently: "Would it help to think about what you would do if things got worse?" If they are open,

encourage professional help (like 1800RESPECT or local DV services) to create a tailored safety plan.

Q: What if both partners are doing some behaviours, even if they are different? Does that mean it is not

abuse?
A: Not necessarily. Conflict and coercive control are very different.

Normal conflict happens in all relationships. Both people might argue, raise their voices, or make mistakes, but it is equal, repair is possible, and no one is systematically afraid of the other. Coercive control is a pattern where one person holds more power. Even if the survivor sometimes yells back, checks a phone, or slams a door out of frustration, this does not mean the relationship is "mutual abuse." Survivors often act in self-defence, desperation, or under pressure.

Professionals look at patterns, intent, and impact. Who is afraid of whom? Who has freedom, and who feels trapped? If one person lives in fear and the other person continues to dominate or intimidate, that is coercive control.

Gentle note: The term "mutual abuse" is misleading. What might appear to be "both sides" is often a response to long-term power imbalances. Survivors are human; they may snap, shout, or act out of exhaustion, but that does not erase the bigger picture.


Q: If it is really abuse, why do I still love them?
A: Trauma bonding and intermittent kindness make it normal to feel love, loyalty, or longing, even when you are being harmed. Love and abuse can coexist in survivors' experiences, but only one of them is healthy.


Q: What if both partners are exhibiting unhealthy behaviours?

A: Relationships under coercive control often become chaotic. Survivors may shout, argue back, or withdraw, but this differs from coercion. The difference lies in pattern and intent: coercive control involves one person establishing and maintaining ongoing power and dominance. Both individuals may exhibit conflictual behaviour, but only one is driving the pattern of fear and control.

Q: They said they have ADHD or anger issues. Does that excuse the abuse?
A: Mental health challenges may explain stress or reactivity, but they never excuse coercive control. Many people live with PTSD or other conditions and never abuse their partners.

Q: Am I overreacting?
A: If you are asking this question, it usually means something feels deeply wrong. Abuse often minimises itself (" not that bad," "Everyone argues"). Trust your body: fear, dread, and walking on eggshells are signals of danger, not overreaction. Abuse thrives when survivors doubt themselves. If someone repeatedly dismisses your feelings, isolates you, or makes you afraid, that is not being "too sensitive"; it is a sign of control.

Q: What if I still love them?
A: Loving someone who hurts you is common. Trauma bonds combine fear and affection, making leaving even more difficult. Love does not erase abuse. Both can coexist, but only one is safe for you and your children.

Q: Will people judge me for staying?

A: Survivors stay for reasons of safety, financial security, children, or hope that things will change. Staying is not a weakness; it is a matter of survival. You deserve compassion, not judgment. Leaving becomes possible when safety and readiness align, not before.

Q: How do I know if it has gone too far or risks escalating?

A: If you notice threats, stalking, physical violence, or if your gut tells you your friend is in immediate danger, trust that instinct. Call emergency services (000 in Australia) if necessary, even if your friend does not want you to. Safety comes first.

Q: My friend says their partner acts that way because they have PTSD, and that is why they lash out and throw things. Is that an excuse?

A: Mental health conditions like PTSD can affect emotions, but they are never an excuse for abusive or controlling behaviour. Many people live with PTSD or trauma without harming others. Abuse is about choice and control, not just "losing it."

Throwing objects, shouting, or intimidating a partner are acts of violence, even if there is no physical hit.

It is crucial to separate understanding (yes, trauma may explain stress or triggers) from accountability (they are still responsible for their behaviour and for seeking healthy coping strategies).

If someone blames PTSD or mental health for abuse, it may be part of gaslighting or shifting responsibility.

Q: Will the authorities take my kids away if I report domestic violence?
A: Reporting DV does not mean you will automatically lose your children. Child protection usually sees the non-violent parent as the protective one. Their role is to work with you to keep children safe, not to punish you. However, misunderstandings occur, so documenting abuse, showing the protective steps you have taken, and getting DV-informed legal advice is essential. You deserve support, not blame.

Q: Will anyone believe me if I speak up?
A: Doubt is a tool of abuse. Abusers often make survivors feel "crazy" or unbelievable. Many professionals understand coercive control, and naming it more often makes dismissal more difficult. Keeping records, seeking support, and trusting your own truth can help counter the fear of not being believed.

# What You Can Do If Someone You Know Is Experiencing Abuse

Family and friends are often the first to notice when something feels wrong. Knowing how to respond can make the difference between silence and safety. You don't need to have all the answers; you need to be a safe and steady presence.

### How to Help Safely (Family & Friends):

Listen without judgment; believe them. Avoid asking, "Why don't you leave?" and instead ask, "How can I support you?"

Affirm their reality; abuse thrives on minimisation and gaslighting. Saying, "What you are experiencing is not okay," can counter the self-doubt survivors carry.

Respect their choices; leaving can be dangerous. Offer support without pushing them before they are ready.

Practical support:

Offer childcare, transport, or a safe place to store essential items.

Help gather information about services or accompany them to appointments if asked.

Stay connected: isolation is one of the abuser's strongest tools. Even small check-ins, such as a text, a coffee, or a reminder that they matter, can be effective.

Know the limits: you cannot rescue someone, and confronting the abuser can escalate risk. The most powerful role you can play is consistent, non-judgmental support.

Be prepared for your loved one to feel angry, defensive, or to deny what you are raising. This is common, and it is not a reflection on you. Survivors are often unaware of the full extent of what is happening to them, and denial can be a powerful coping mechanism. By speaking up, you may plant a seed — and sometimes that seed takes time to grow. Some survivors may not be ready to face the truth right away, and that is okay. (Be kind to yourself and reach out for support if you need to. It is hard to be a bystander, feeling helpless.

If someone is in immediate danger:

Call emergency services (000 in Australia).

Do not intervene if it puts you at risk of physical harm.

**Remember:**
Supporting someone through abuse is about walking beside them, not leading or pushing. Your role is to hold hope when they cannot, and to remind them they are not alone.


### For Professionals

Teachers, doctors, lawyers, social workers, and frontline responders often encounter survivors in moments of crisis or disclosure. The way you respond can either build trust or deepen the silence.

Recommended methods:

Name the behaviour clearly: use terms like coercive control or abuse, not just relationship problems. Naming validates the survivor's experience.

Document patterns, not just incidents: Courts and systems respond more strongly when there is a simple record of repeated behaviour.

Stay neutral but compassionate: avoid minimising or adopting the abuser's narrative. Simple statements like 'It is reasonable that you are concerned about safety' can ground survivors.

When referring for safety after disclosure, do not insist on mediation or joint counselling. These settings can be unsafe and re-traumatise survivors.

Confidentiality and caution: Abusers may monitor phones, emails, or even children's school bags. Share information discreetly and with survivor consent.

Offer choices, not directives: Empower survivors by presenting safe options (" Here are services that can help...") rather than issuing commands.

**Remember:**
Professionals are often gatekeepers to safety. You can be a catalyst for someone. A trauma-informed, non-judgmental response can break through years of silence and shame and may be the step that allows a survivor to reach out for help.

# The Butterfly Metaphor

For much of this book, we have explored survival in the storms, the waves, the moments when your body and mind were holding on. However, healing is about surviving. It is also about transforming.

A butterfly begins life as a caterpillar, small and earthbound. When the time comes, it retreats into a cocoon, a place that looks still on the outside but is full of invisible change inside. In the quiet, the caterpillar dissolves and reorganises into something new. When it emerges, it carries wings.

Healing from coercive control can lead to entering a cocoon. At first, it may resemble collapse, shutdown, or deep rest—a stage where it seems as if nothing is. However, beneath the surface, your nervous system, your sense of self, and your spirit are quietly relearning.

The butterfly does not rush its wings open. It waits, gathering the strength to fly. Similarly, recovery unfolds at its own pace. Each small step—a day of rest, a moment of laughter, a boundary honoured—is part of your wings taking shape.

And just as the butterfly never returns to being a caterpillar.

Survival and transformation are inseparable parts of the same story.

## To the Reader

If you have stayed, if you are not yet ready to leave, or if you are somewhere in between, please know this: I am proud of you. It's not about me though it's about you! And I hope you are proud of yourselves!!! You have shown courage to read these words, to sit with brutal truths, and to let yourself hope for something different. Readiness does not happen on anyone else's timetable. Wherever you are right now, you are not alone in this world.

## To the Professionals

If you are reading this as a professional in law, social work, health, education, or any other field, thank you. Thank you for taking the time to understand, for listening, and for creating a space where survivors often feel heard. The role you play is significant: the words you choose, the patience you show, and the willingness to see patterns of coercive control can change the course of someone's life. Please carry this knowledge forward, not only as information but as compassion in action.

Every ending is also a beginning. May this not just mark the last page, but serve as an invitation to imagine, to heal, and to start a new chapter in your book.

With love, kindness, and a heart full of blessings sent your way.

Bec xxx

I've been on quite a journey getting this book to print — it's felt like a full-blown nightmare! Since a publisher published my first book, they took care of the formatting, layout, and sizing This time, I took it all on myself because I wanted to share this message without delay.

By chance, I attended the book launch of a woman I once served with on a council committee. We crossed paths again, and she generously shared the details of a self-publisher. That moment opened new doors — and since then, so much has unfolded.

I'm deeply honoured and excited to share that we've now secured government sponsorship for an e-petition to reform legislation in Tasmania. I am profoundly grateful to the Members of Parliament who took the time to respond, and especially to The Honourable Ruth Forrest for graciously agreeing to sponsor the petition. I would also like to acknowledge The Honourable Rebecca (Bec) Jane Thomas for her support in following up with the Governor-General and helping ensure that this vital work continues.

This journey has required me to sit deeply within my story. One of my children loves the artist Jelly Roll — whose music has also been a powerful source of healing and connection for me. I bought tickets to two of his Australian shows, hoping that by the time he arrived, perhaps the surrounding systems might have stepped in to bring some peace and change.

That day, I truly believed God was working through Jelly Roll. Out of a crowd of people, he noticed the photo of one of my children that I wore around my neck and gently asked about them. There may have been some misunderstanding afterward, and I've tried to reach out to clarify — but what mattered most was that, in that brief and sacred moment, I could share a small piece of my story and the love I hold for my beautiful child, even while being limited in what I can say publicly.

That night, I learnt that Jelly Roll is the real deal — authentic, compassionate, and deeply human. There was something in his eyes, a quiet understanding that words couldn't capture. It meant the world to me to show him my matching tattoo of the cross and to share, even for a moment, how precious my baby truly is.

Sometimes the ones you never imagined... truly hear you.

Sharing the love within my heart.

We are all battling something—each of us carrying our own story of pain and hope. But when we stand together with kindness and compassion, we are stronger.

RiseKindCo™— because there is strength in kindness, and we rise stronger together.

# Resources and Support Organisations

Finding reliable resources and support organisations is crucial for individuals and families affected by domestic and family violence. This appendix provides a list of services in Australia and internationally to help survivors navigate these challenging situations.

**Gentle Note:** This list is not exhaustive. I apologise if I have missed any vital services.

Emergency Services (Australia)

Police, Fire, Ambulance: Dial 000 (for immediate danger or emergencies)

## Key Support Services (Australia)

1800RESPECT: 1800 737 732

National sexual assault, domestic and family violence counselling service (24/7)

Lifeline: 13 11 14

Crisis support and suicide prevention (24/7).

Beyond Blue: 1300 224 636

Support for anxiety, depression, and mental health (24/7).

Relationships Australia: 1300 364 277

Counselling, mediation, and support services nationwide.

Men's Referral Service: 1300 766 491

Kids Helpline: 1800 551 800

Family Relationship Advice Line
1800 050 321 | familyrelationships.gov.au

International Support Lines

International Emergency: Dial the local emergency number (e.g., 911 in the USA, 112 in the EU/UK).

National Domestic Violence Hotline (USA): 1-800-799-SAFE

UK National Domestic Abuse Helpline: 0808 2000 247

New Zealand–Women's Refuge Crisis Line: 0800 733 843

## Reference List

Adams, A. E., Sullivan, C. M., Bybee, D., & Greeson, M. R. (2008). Development of the scale of economic abuse. Violence Against Women, 14(5), 563–588. https://doi.org/10.1177/1077801208315529

Adelaide Now. (2023, October 30). 'Forever changed': DV survivor hopes to break cycle after horror abuse. News Corp Australia.

Aharoni, E., & Vincent, G. M. (2023). Neuroprediction of violence and criminal behavior using neuroimaging. Neuroscience & Biobehavioral Reviews, 155, 105423. https://doi.org/10.1016/j.neubiorev.2023.105423

Anderson, C. A., & Bushman, B. J. (2018). Media violence and the general aggression model. Journal of Social Issues, 74(2), 386–413. https://doi.org/10.1111/josi.12275

Astridge Clarke, A. D., Copas, C., Hannon, O., Padgett, C., Makovec Knight, J., Falkenberg, A., Varto, H., Mason, K., Wellington, C. L., van Donkelaar, P., Marks, J., Shultz, S. R., & Symons, G. F. (2024). Detecting a hidden pandemic: the current state and future direction of screening and assessment tools for intimate partner violence-related brain injury. Neuroscience & Biobehavioral Reviews, 167, 105912. https://doi.org/10.1016/j.neubiorev.2024.105912

Assor, A., Roth, G., & Deci, E. L. (2004). The emotional costs of parents' conditional regard: A self-determination theory analysis. Journal of Personality, 72(2), 47–88. https://doi.org/10.1111/j.0022-3506.2004.00256.x

Australian Institute of Family Studies. (2023). Coercive control literature review: final report. Melbourne, Australia: Australian Institute of Family Studies. http://nla.gov.au/nla.obj-3220000428

Australian Law Reform Commission. (2010). Family violence — a national legal response: alrc report 114. Commonwealth of Australia. https://www.alrc.gov.au/publication/family-violence-a-national-legal-response-alrc-report-114

Australian Institute of Family Studies (AIFS). (2023). Coercive control: Implications for practitioners and service responses. Commonwealth of Australia. https://aifs.gov.au

Australian Capital Television Pty Ltd v Commonwealth (1992) 177 CLR 106.

Australian Law Reform Commission. (2019). Family law for the future – An inquiry into the family law system (Report No. 135). Commonwealth of Australia.

Australian Institute of Family Studies. (2023). *What the research evidence tells us about coercive control victimisation.* https://aifs.gov.au

Australian Institute of Family Studies. (2015). *Children's exposure to domestic and family violence: Key issues and responses* (CFCA Paper No. 36). https://aifs.gov.au

Australian National University. (2023, January 30). Coercive control takes significant toll on children. ANU News. https://www.anu.edu.au/news/all-news/coercive-control-takes-significant-toll-on-children

Arnsten, A. F. T. (2009). Stress signalling pathways that impair prefrontal cortex structure and function.

Nature Reviews Neuroscience, 10(6), 410–422. https://doi.org/10.1038/nrn2648

Australian National University. (2024). The mental health impacts of coercive control on children and young people. Centre for Social Research and Methods, Australian National University.

Adelaide Company of Jehovah's Witnesses Inc v Commonwealth (1943) 67 CLR 116.

Bancroft, L. (2002). Why does he do that? inside the minds of angry and controlling men. New York: Berkley Books.

Bancroft, L., & Silverman, J. G. (2002). The batterer as parent: Addressing the impact of domestic violence on family dynamics. Thousand Oaks, CA: Sage Publications.

Batty, R., & Corbett, B. (2015). Rosie batty: a mother's story. HarperCollins.

Barber, B. K. (1996). Parental psychological control: Revisiting a neglected construct. Child Development, 67(6), 3296–3319. https://doi.org/10.2307/1131780

Bechara, A., Damasio, H., & Damasio, A. R. (2000). Emotion, decision making and the orbitofrontal cortex. Cerebral Cortex, 10(3), 295–307. https://doi.org/10.1093/cercor/10.3.295

Benstead, U. (2024). The Shark Cage Framework: Empowering women and girls to recognise and protect their right to safety and respect. The Shark Cage. https://thesharkcage.com/about/about-the-shark-cage-framework/

Benstead, U. (2024). The Shark Cage Program. https://www.ursulabenstead.com.au

Bisson, J. I., Roberts, N. P., Andrew, M., Cooper, R., & Lewis, C. (2013). Psychological therapies for chronic post-traumatic stress disorder (ptsd) in adults. Cochrane Database of Systematic Reviews, 2013(12), Article CD003388. https://doi.org/10.1002/14651858.CD003388.pub4

Blair, R. J. R. (2001). Neurocognitive models of aggression, the antisocial personality disorders, and psychopathy. Journal of Neurology, Neurosurgery & Psychiatry, 71(6), 727–731. https://doi.org/10.1136/jnnp.71.6.727

Blair, R. J. R. (2016). The neurobiology of aggression and violence. Current Opinion in Psychology, 11, 123–128. https://doi.org/10.1016/j.copsyc.2016.06.007

Blair, R. J. R. (2013). The neurobiology of psychopathic traits in youths. Nature Reviews Neuroscience, 14(11), 786–799. https://doi.org/10.1038/nrn3577

Bowlby, J. (1969). Attachment and loss: vol. 1. Attachment. New York, NY: Basic Books.

Bowlby, J. (1988). A secure base: parent-child attachment and healthy human development. New York, NY: Basic Books.

Brown, B. (2010). The gifts of imperfection. Hazelden.

Button, D. M. (2009). Training child protective services workers about domestic violence: needs, strategies, and barriers. Children & Youth Services Review, 31(3), 315–321.

Carnes, P. (1997). The betrayal bond: breaking free of exploitive relationships. Deerfield Beach, FL: Health Communications.

Chapman, G. (Year). The 5 Love Languages: The Secret to Love that Lasts. Northfield Publishing.

Children Australia (Journal). (2024). *Coercive control and situational couple violence in families with child protection involvement* (Article 3008). https://childrenaustralia.org.au

Decety, J., Chen, C., Harenski, C., & Kiehl, K. A. (2013). An fmri study of affective perspective taking in individuals with psychopathy. Frontiers in Human Neuroscience, 7, 489. https://doi.org/10.3389/fnhum.2013.00489

Decety, J., Chen, C., Harenski, C., & Kiehl, K. A. (2013). An fMRI study of affective perspective taking in individuals with psychopathy: Imagining another in pain does not evoke empathy. Frontiers in Human Neuroscience, 7, 489. https://doi.org/10.3389/fnhum.2013.00489

Delaney Roberts Family Lawyers — Understanding the Intersection between Coercive Control and Family Law (2024).

Dettenborn, L., Tietze, A., Kirschbaum, C., & Stalder, T. (2012). The assessment of cortisol in human hair: a biomarker of chronic stress. Psychoneuroendocrinology, 37(10), 1661–1670. https://doi.org/10.1016/j.psyneuen.2011.11.003

Dobash, R. E., & Dobash, R. P. (2004). Women's violence to men in intimate relationships: working on a puzzle. British Journal of Criminology, 44(3), 324–349. https://doi.org/10.1093/bjc/azh026

Douglas, H. (2018). Legal systems abuse and coercive control. Criminology & Criminal Justice, 18(1), 84–99. https://doi.org/10.1177/1748895817728380

☐ Douglas, H., & Fell, B. (2022). Coercive control in Australia: Family law, criminal law and protecting women and children. Melbourne University Law Review, 46(2), 499–536.

Drury, J., & Easteal, P. (2021). Fathers' allegations of mental health and mothers' allegations of coercive control. Australian Journal of Family Law, 34(1), 57–90.

Drury, J., & Easteal, P. (2021). Fathers' allegations of mental health and mothers' allegations of coercive control: intersections and outcomes in family law proceedings. Australian Journal of Family Law, 34(1), 57–90.

Dwyer, P., Scullion, L., Jones, K., & McNeill, J. (2018). Welfare conditionality. Routledge.

Erikson, E. H. (1968). Identity: Youth and crisis. W. W. Norton.

Elizabeth, V. (2017). Custody stalking: a mechanism of coercively controlling mothers following separation. Feminist Legal Studies, 25(2), 185–201. https://doi.org/10.1007/s10691-017-9349-9

Fabian, J. M. (2025). Forensic neuroscience and violence. Wiley-Blackwell.

Family Law Act 1975 (Cth) s 121.

Federal Circuit and Family Court of Australia — The Lighthouse Project: Two Years Later (Voice Lawyers summary, 2023-2024).

Ferguson, C. J., & Beaver, K. M. (2009). Natural born killers: the genetic origins of extreme violence. Aggression and Violent Behavior, 14(5), 286–294. https://doi.org/10.1016/j.avb.2009.03.005

Ford, J. D., Spinazzola, J., van der Kolk, B. A., & Grasso, D. J. (2013). Toward an empirically based developmental trauma disorder diagnosis for children: Factor structure, reliability, and validity of the Developmental Trauma Disorder Semi-structured Interview. Journal of Clinical Psychiatry, 74(8), 841–849. https://doi.org/10.4088/JCP.12m08030

Foster, J. A., & Neufeld, K. A. M. (2013). Gut–brain axis: how the microbiome influences anxiety and depression. Trends in Neurosciences, 36(5), 305–312. https://doi.org/10.1016/j.tins.2013.01.005

Forward, S., & Frazier, D. (1997). Emotional blackmail: When the people in your life use fear, obligation, and guilt to manipulate you. HarperCollins Publishers.

Framing the Narrative. (2025, April 16). It's all in your head: The untold cost of coercive control on Australian women.

Freyd, J. J. (1997). Violations of power, adaptive blindness, and betrayal trauma theory. Feminism & Psychology, 7(1), 22–32. https://doi.org/10.1177/0959353597071004

Freyd, J. J., & Smidt, A. M. (2019). Darvo: deny, attack, and reverse victim and offender. Journal of Aggression, Maltreatment & Trauma, 28(4), 467–477. https://doi.org/10.1080/10926771.2018.1527891

García-Vergara, S., Alegría, M., Wong, J., & Fallon, B. (2022). Risk assessment instruments for intimate partner femicide: a systematic review. Frontiers in Psychology, 13, 896901. https://doi.org/10.3389/fpsyg.2022.896901

Gleeson, H. (2021, September 17). Rosie Batty joins family violence experts' calls to prioritise preventing coercive control. ABC News.

Goldstein, A. N., & Walker, M. P. (2014). The role of sleep in emotional brain function. Annual Review of Clinical Psychology, 10, 679–708.

https://doi.org/10.1146/annurev-clinpsy-032813-153716

Goldstein, R. Z., & Volkow, N. D. (2011). Dysfunction of the prefrontal cortex in addiction. Nature Reviews Neuroscience, 12(11), 652–669.

Goodman, L. A., Thomas, K., Cattaneo, L. B., Heimel, D., Woulfe, J., & Chong, S. K. (2016). Survivor-defined practice in domestic violence work. Journal of Interpersonal Violence, 31(1), 163–185. https://doi.org/10.1177/0886260514555131

Goroff, N. N. (1974). Social welfare as coercive social control. The Journal of Sociology & Social Welfare, 2(1), 3–12.

Graham, D. L. R., Rawlings, E., & Rigsby, R. K. (1994). Loving to survive: sexual terror, men's violence, and women's lives. New York: New York University Press.

Hanna, C. (2009). The paradox of progress: translating evan stark's coercive control into legal doctrine for abused women. Violence Against Women, 15(12), 1458–1476. https://doi.org/10.1177/1077801209347091

Herman, J. L. (2015). Trauma and recovery: The aftermath of violence—from domestic abuse to political terror. Basic Books.

Hill, J. (2020). See what you made me do: power, control and domestic abuse. Black Inc.

Hooper, L. M. (2007). Expanding the discussion regarding parentification and its varied outcomes: Implications for mental health research and practice. Journal of Mental Health Counseling, 29(4), 322–337.

https://doi.org/10.17744/mehc.29.4.5cxm4h4p6h5p
8468

Jacka, F. N., O'Neil, A., Opie, R., Itsiopoulos, C., Cotton, S., Mohebbi, M., Castle, D., Dash, S., Mihalopoulos, C.,

Chatterton, M. L., Brazionis, L., Dean, O. M., Hodge, A. M., & Berk, M. (2017). A randomised controlled trial of dietary improvement for adults with major depression. BMC Medicine, 15(1), 23. https://doi.org/10.1186/s12916-017-0791-y

Jagasia, E., et al. (2023). A systematic literature review of protective factors mitigating the effects of children's exposure to IPV. *Journal of Advanced Nursing*. https://onlinelibrary.wiley.com

Jakovljevic, M., Lepojevic, V., & Stanisavljevic, D. (2022). A model of coercive control in higher education: A qualitative study. F1000Research, 11, 880. https://doi.org/10.12688/f1000research.122154.1

Kabat-Zinn, J. (1994). Wherever you go, there you are. Hyperion.

Katz, E. (2022). Coercive control in children's and mothers' lives. Oxford University Press.

Kelly, J. B., & Johnson, M. P. (2008). Differentiation among types of intimate partner violence. Family Court Review, 46(3), 476–499. https://doi.org/10.1111/j.1744-1617.2008.00215.x

Katz, E. (2016). Beyond the physical incident model: How children living with domestic violence are harmed by and resist regimes of coercive control. Child Abuse Review, 25(1), 46–59. https://doi.org/10.1002/car.2422

Kelly, J. B., & Johnson, M. P. (2008). Differentiation among types of intimate partner violence. Family Court Review, 46(3), 476–499. https://doi.org/10.1111/j.1744-1617.2008.00215.x

Kelly, L., & Westmarland, N. (2016). Naming and defining 'domestic violence':Lessons from research with violent men. Feminist Review, 112(1), 113–127. https://doi.org/10.1057/fr.2015.52

Kelly, L. (1988). Surviving sexual violence. University of Minnesota Press.

Kelly, L., Sharp-Jeffs, N., & Klein, R. (2014). Finding the costs of freedom. Solace Women's Aid.

Koob, G. F., & Volkow, N. D. (2016). Neurobiology of addiction: A neurocircuitry analysis. The Lancet Psychiatry, 3(8), 760–773. https://doi.org/10.1016/S2215-0366(16)00104-8

Kraft, C., & Mayeux, L. (2018). Associations among friendship jealousy, peer status, and relational aggression in early adolescence. The Journal of Early Adolescence, 38(2), 227–244. https://doi.org/10.1177/0272431616670999

Laing, L. (2017). Secondary victimisation: domestic violence survivors navigating the family law system. Violence Against Women, 23(11), 1314–1335. https://doi.org/10.1177/1077801216659942

.Lamont, A., & Price-Robertson, R. (2024). Child protection and coercive control: Emerging practice insights. Australian Institute of Family Studies.

Lamont, A., & Price-Robertson, R. (2024). Kids are in the middle of it – child protection practitioners reflect on domestic and family violence and coercive control. Children and Youth Services Review, 156, 107397. https://doi.org/10.1016/j.childyouth.2024.107397

Lancet Public Health. (2024). Interventions that prevent or respond to IPV and VAC by parents/caregivers: Systematic review of components and mechanisms. *The Lancet Public Health.* https://www.thelancet.com

Lange v Australian Broadcasting Corporation (1997) 189 CLR 520

Levine, P. A. (1997). Waking the tiger. North Atlantic Books.

Levine, P. A. (2010). In an unspoken voice. North Atlantic Books.

Marshall, R., Warburton, W., Kangas, M., & Sweller, N. (2025). Internet gaming disorder and smartphone overuse in australian children. Current Psychology. https://doi.org/10.1007/s12144-025-07975-w

Matthewson, M., & Sillars, A. (2023, June 13). EMMM submission: Family Law Amendment Bill 2023. Eeny Meeny Miney Mo Foundation. https://emmm.org.au/submissions

Marwitz, U., Higgins, D. J., & Whelan, T. (2024). Coercive control and situational couple violence in families. Children Australia, 46(2), Article 3008. https://doi.org/10.61605/cha_3008

Matwitz, K., Higgins, D. J., & Whelan, J. (2024). Assessing coercive control in family law and child protection cases: Challenges and opportunities. University of Melbourne / Australian Institute of Family Studies.

McLeod, D., & Flood, S. (2018). *Coercive control: Impacts on children and young people in the family environment* (Review). Research in Practice / SafeLives. https://adultsdp.researchinpractice.org.uk/media/yb

kc4pea/coercive control impacts on children and young people in the family environment literature review 2018.pdf

McEwen, B. S. (2017). Neurobiological and systemic effects of chronic stress. Chronic Stress, 1, 1–11. https://doi.org/10.1177/2470547017692328

Meaney, M. J. (2010). Epigenetics and the biological definition of gene × environment interactions. Child Development, 81(1), 41–79. https://doi.org/10.1111/j.1467-8624.2009.01381.x

Mahoney, M. R. (1991). Legal images of battered women: Redefining the issue of separation. Michigan Law Review, 90(1), 1–68. https://doi.org/10.2307/1289740

Mikulincer, M., & Shaver, P. R. (2007). Attachment in adulthood: Structure, dynamics, and change. Guilford Press.

Murray, C. E., Crowe, A., & Akers, W. (2015). How can we end the cycle of violence? Journal of the Society for Social Work and Research, 6(3), 369–393.

Namnyak, M., Tufton, N., Szekely, R., Toal, M., Worboys, S., & Sampson, E. L. (2008). 'stockholm syndrome': psychiatric diagnosis or urban myth? acta psychiatrica scandinavica, 117(1), 4–11. https://doi.org/10.1111/j.1600-0447.2007.01112.x

National Domestic and Family Violence Bench Book (2024 Update). Australasian Institute of Judicial Administration / SouthSafe.

Neff, K. D. (2003). The development and validation of a scale to measure self-compassion. Self and Identity, 2(3), 223–250. https://doi.org/10.1080/15298860309067

Neff, K. D. (2011). Self-compassion. William Morrow.

NSPCC. (2023). *Helplines insight briefing: The impact of coercive control on children and young people.* NSPCC. https://learning.nspcc.org.uk/research-resources/2023/impact-coercive-control-children-young-people

Pasalich, D., Xyrakis, N., Aquilina, B., McNiece, E., Tran, T., Waddell, C., Suomi, A., & others. (2022). *Interparental coercive control and child and family outcomes: A systematic review. Trauma, Violence, & Abuse.* https://doi.org/10.1177/15248380221139243

Petronio, S. (2002). Boundaries of privacy: Dialectics of disclosure. SUNY Press.

Pence, E., & Paymar, M. (1993). Education groups for men who batter: the duluth model. Springer Publishing Company.

Perry, B. D. (2009). Examining child maltreatment through a neurodevelopmental lens. Journal of Loss and Trauma, 14(4), 240–255. https://doi.org/10.1080/15325020903004350

*Pickford v Pickford* [2024] FedCFamC1A 249 (Austl.).

Federal Circuit and Family Court of Australia (Division 1) (Full Court).

Pitman, T. (2024). Tangled web of words: A breakthrough guide to conversational and coercive control in relationships. TalkingWise

Porges, S. W. (2011). The polyvagal theory. W. W. Norton & Company.

Promising Futures / Futures Without Violence. (2018). *Comprehensive review of interventions for children exposed to domestic violence* (updated). https://promising.futureswithoutviolence.org

Quancai, M., Meng, L., & Kunjie, J. (2023). Social control and self-control: domestic violence and adolescents' internet gaming addiction. Frontiers in Psychiatry, 14, 1245563. https://doi.org/10.3389/fpsyt.2023.1245563

Quinlan, F., Donnelly, S., & O'Donnell, D. (2024). Coercive control of older adults in filial relationships: A hybrid concept analysis. The Journal of Adult Protection, 26(6), 279–295. Emerald. https://doi.org/10.1108/JAP-06-2024-0033

Quancai, M., Meng, L., & Kunjie, J. (2023). Social control and self-control: factors linking exposure to domestic violence and adolescents' internet gaming addiction. Frontiers in Psychiatry, 14, 1245563. https://doi.org/10.3389/fpsyt.2023.1245563

Qualitative CP practitioner study (Australia). (2024). *"Kids are in the middle of it' – Child protection practitioners reflect..." Children and Youth Services Review.* https://sciencedirect.com

Quinlan, C., Donnelly, M., & O'Donnell, D. (2024). Conceptualising filial coercive control: Towards a model of elder abuse in adult–child relationships. Journal of Adult Protection, 26(2), 75–92. https://doi.org/10.1108/JAP-08-2023-0024

Raine, A. (2013). The anatomy of violence: The biological roots of crime. New York, NY: Pantheon.

Rathus, Z. (2020). A history of the use of the concept of parental alienation in the australian family law system: contradictions, collisions and their consequences. Journal of Social Welfare & Family Law, 42(1), 5–17. (Open-access on Griffith repository.)

Richie, B. E. (2012). Arrested justice: black women, violence, and america's prison nation. NYU Press.

Rollero, C., & De Piccoli, N. (2020). Myths about intimate partner violence and moral disengagement. International Journal of Environmental Research and Public Health, 17(21), 8139.

Sapolsky, R. M. (2015). Stress and the brain: Individual variability and the inverted-U. Nature Neuroscience, 18(10), 1344–1346. https://doi.org/10.1038/nn.4109

Soenens, B., & Vansteenkiste, M. (2010). A theoretical upgrade of the concept of parental psychological control: Proposing new insights on the basis of self-determination theory. Developmental Review, 30(1), 74–99. https://doi.org/10.1016/j.dr.2009.11.001

SafeSpace Counselling Services. (n.d.). Why doesn't she leave?

SAFER Resource. (n.d.). Why don't victims just leave?

Sánchez-Villegas, A., Henríquez-Sánchez, P., Ruiz-Canela, M., Lahortiga, F., Molero, P., Toledo, E., & Martínez-González, M. A. (2015). A longitudinal analysis of diet quality scores and the risk of incident depression in the SUN Project. BMC Medicine, 13, 197. https://doi.org/10.1186/s12916-015-0428-y

Shadows of Control. (2023). Victim blaming comments: why victim blaming isharmful and what it sounds like. Shadows of Control. https://shadowsofcontrol.com/articles/victim-blaming-comments/

Shapiro, F. (2017). Eye movement desensitization and reprocessing (emdr) therapy: basic principles, protocols, and procedures (3rd ed.). Guilford Press.

Siegel, D. J. (2020). The developing mind (3rd ed.). Guilford Press.

Siegel, D. J. (2020). The developing mind: how relationships and the brain interact to shape who we are (3rd ed.). Guilford Press.

Sillars, A. (2017, October 2). Children forced to take sides face emotional crisis: The child as weapon in family court process. Eeny Meeny Miney Mo Foundation. https://www.academia.edu/64143810/Children_For ced_to_Take_Sides_Face_Emotional_Crisis

Skinner, B. F. (1953). Science and human behavior. Macmillan.

Skylar. (2012, June 13). The gray rock method of dealing with psychopaths. 180rule.com. https://180rule.com/the-gray-rock-method-of-dealing-with-psychopaths/

Social Ventures Australia. Evaluation Report – Lighthouse Project (Greater Shepparton) 2023.

Sokoloff, N. J., & Dupont, I. (2005). Domestic violence at the intersections of race, class, and gender. Violence Against Women, 11(1), 38–64.

Stark, E. (2007). Coercive control: how men entrap women in personal life. Oxford University Press.

Stark, E. (2023). Children of coercive control: The impact of domestic abuse on children. Oxford University Press.

Storey, J. E. (2020). Risk factors for elder abuse and neglect: A review of the literature. Aggression and Violent Behavior, 50, 101339. https://doi.org/10.1016/j.avb.2019.101339

Sullivan, C. M., & Bybee, D. I. (1999). Reducing violence using community-based advocacy for women with abusive partners. Journal of Consulting and Clinical Psychology, 67(1), 43–53.

Sweet, P. L. (2019). The sociology of gaslighting. American Sociological Review, 84(5), 851–875. https://doi.org/10.1177/0003122419874843

Tedeschi, R. G., & Calhoun, L. G. (2004). Posttraumatic growth: Conceptual foundations and empirical evidence. Psychological Inquiry, 15(1), 1–18. https://doi.org/10.1207/s15327965pli1501_01

The National Principles to Address Coercive Control in Family and Domestic Violence (2023). Standing Council of Attorneys-General.

Tolmie, J. (2018). Coercive control: To criminalize or not to criminalize? Criminology & Criminal Justice, 18(1), 50–66.

University of Queensland. (2025, September 3). Coercive control puts children at risk of mental illness later in life.

University of Queensland. (2025). Children's mental health and coercive control: Evidence summary. School of Psychology, The University of Queensland.

van der Kolk, B. A. (2014). The body keeps the score: Brain, mind, and body in the healing of trauma. New York, NY: Viking.

Van IJzendoorn, M. H., & Bakermans-Kranenburg, M. J. (2015). Genetic differential susceptibility on trial. Development and Psychopathology, 27(1), 151–162. https://doi.org/10.1017/S0954579414001369

Volkow, N. D., & Morales, M. (2015). The brain on drugs: from reward to addiction. Cell, 162(4), 712–725. https://doi.org/10.1016/j.cell.2015.07.046

Walker, J. (2013). Complex ptsd: from surviving to thriving. Azure Coyote.

Walklate, S., Fitz-Gibbon, K., & McCulloch, J. (2018). Is more law the answer? criminology & criminal justice, 18(1), 115–131. https://doi.org/10.1177/1748895817728561

Wallace & Wallace Lawyers — What is the Lighthouse Project and the Evatt List? (2024).

Weinstein, A. (2020). Neurobiological mechanisms underlying internet gaming disorder. Dialogues in Clinical Neuroscience, 22(2), 139–146. https://doi.org/10.31887/DCNS.2020.22.2/aweinstein

Wilcox, P. (2006). Surviving domestic violence. Palgrave Macmillan.

Wilcox, P. (2006). Surviving domestic violence: gender, poverty and agency. Palgrave Macmillan.

Wilson, M., & Daly, M. (1993). Spousal homicide risk and estrangement. Violence and Victims, 8(1), 3–16. https://doi.org/10.1891/0886-6708.8.1.3

Woodlock, D. (2017). The abuse of technology in domestic violence and stalking. Violence Against Women, 23(5), 584–602. https://doi.org/10.1177/1077801216646277

Yehuda, R., Daskalakis, N. P., Bierer, L. M., Bader, H. N., Klengel, T., Holsboer, F., & Binder, E. B. (2016). Holocaust exposure induced intergenerational effects on fkbp5 methylation. Biological Psychiatry, 80(5), 372–380. https://doi.org/10.1016/j.biopsych.2015.08.005

Yu, R., Molero, Y., Lichtenstein, P., Larsson, H., Prescott-Mayling, C., Howard, L. M., & Fazel, S. (2023). Development and validation of a prediction tool for reoffending risk in individuals arrested for domestic violence. JAMA Network Open, 6(7), e2325494. https://doi.org/10.1001/jamanetworkopen.2023.25494

Zeidan, F., Johnson, S. K., Diamond, B. J., David, Z., & Goolkasian, P. (2010). Mindfulness meditation improves cognition. Consciousness and Cognition, 19(2), 597–605.

Zahr, N. M., & Pfefferbaum, A. (2017). Alcohol's effects on the brain: Neuroimaging results in humans and animal models. Alcohol Research: Current Reviews, 38(2), 183–206.